COUNTRY
RAG
CRAFTS

COUNTRY
RAG
CRAFTS

SUE REEVES

David & Charles

To Gordon West

A DAVID & CHARLES BOOK

Copyright text and drawings © Sue Reeves 1996
First published 1996 Copyright photography and layout
© David & Charles 1996

A catalogue record for this book is available from the British
Library.

ISBN 0 7153 0290 6

Typeset by ABM Typographics Ltd, Hull
and printed in Italy by LEGO SpA
for David & Charles
Brunel House Newton Abbot Devon

Contents

INTRODUCTION 6

COLLECTING AND PREPARING RAGS 8

RAG RUGS 18

COILED, CROCHETED AND KNITTED RUGS 28

WEAVING WITH FABRIC 40

DECORATIVE ROOM FURNISHINGS 48

GREETINGS CARDS 58

DECORATIVE WREATHS AND RINGS 66

DECORATIVE HOUSEHOLD OBJECTS 80

BEADS, BUTTONS AND JEWELLERY 90

RE-USING KNITWEAR 102

DYEING, PRINTING AND MARBLING 110

INDEX 120

Introduction

The idea of creating 'something out of nothing' with fabric is not a new one, but has been rather limited to the art of appliqué, patchwork and rag rug-making. In medieval Europe, patchwork was often used for dresses, wall hangings and ecclesiastical decorations. During the seventeenth and eighteenth centuries in Britain, sumptuous colourful silks and patterned cottons were imported from the East and used to create patchwork quilts. This was a rather genteel pastime for upper-class women, but the work was highly esteemed. Once silks and cottons became affordable, and common enough to be used before they were worn out, patchworking became a more popular craft.

Rag rug-making was very much a working-class tradition in Britain. It used tough, practical materials, was hard on the hands and taken up through necessity and need. The craft was predominant in the north-east of England where easy access to local mills and cloth factories provided a broad variety of woollen materials. The creation of the mat was often a whole family effort, with the children cutting up old woollen coats and blankets into strips, while older members of the household hooked and prodded them through old sacks. Occasionally, prize rugs would be displayed on the table, but sadly, many rag rugs, by their very nature, were used until completely worn and threadbare.

Although patchworking and rag rug-making have been known in Britain and Europe for centuries, both crafts became more artistically developed in America. The European immigrants who settled in the north-east, particularly the Dutch and German settlers, were not wealthy people but used the skills and materials available to them to create beautiful patchwork quilts and rag rugs, amongst many other decorative folk works. Patchwork designs arose out of the need to re-use fabrics for quilts, and strong geometric patterns were the most common designs. Today in America, patchworking has evolved into a highly respected art form, and new designs show complicated and highly technical work.

Hooked rag rugs and plaited mats have a strong tradition in America. Subject matter varied from region to region and state to state; thus rigged schooners are more apparent in Maine, while domestic themes or farm animals dominate further inland. Rugs that have survived from America's early history have become much prized collectors' items.

Although patchwork and rug-making techniques are used frequently throughout the book, you will find other techniques such as weaving, dyeing and printing that are not historically associated with rag crafts. Using traditional techniques in new ways is always an exciting venture, and will usually lead to innovative and beautiful work.

Recent years have seen a resurgence in thrift crafts, and a renewed pleasure in recycling. The fascination and satisfaction of creating something useful and individual from rag-bag pieces, the handling of such a variety of colourful fabrics and textures, and the memories revived by the different pieces – all these add to the craft's charm and appeal. There is an enormous pleasure to be found in hunting for old and unwanted materials; the promise of so much drives you on and the projects you can create from rags are so varied!

For example, you can cut your rags into strips and wind them into colourful balls. Fill a basket with these richly textured balls to keep as a constant inspiration. Or use the projects throughout the book to furnish your home. Hooked or coiled rugs add a simple folk appeal to a room, whether placed by the hearth or draped over a chair or sofa. Decorate furniture with fabric motifs, or add richly textured wreaths and hangings to walls. Create cushions from exotic and sumptuous woven rags, or a blanket from a patchwork of earthy muted woollen scraps.

Make fabric and woollen cards to send, frame or use as a pinboard display to blend with the country, ethnic or period style of a room. Maybe begin on a small scale, with pieces of simple jewellery or greetings cards. Or dive straight in and try your hand at a rag rug! The simplicity of the techniques and the easy availability of such exciting materials ensures that the exploration of rag craft will be a creative and enjoyable experience for years to come.

Collecting and Preparing Rags

The pleasure of creating beautiful objects from discarded clothing is almost equalled by the thrill of searching for the fabric itself. The greater your collection of fabric, the more scope you will have for projects and the easier it will be to find the perfect colours to use together. There is no need to go to great expense – your collection will quickly grow from trips to jumble sales and a turn out of the contents of your own wardrobes.

SOURCING FABRICS

Initially, the best place to begin looking for fabrics to use is your own home. This will give you a good excuse for clearing out cupboards and wardrobes; instead of taking your old clothing to a charity shop, you now have a new reason for hanging onto them. You can be happy in the knowledge that you are not going to lose a favourite piece, simply recycle it! And don't forget your friends who may be sentimentally hoarding some wonderful old clothes but who would be delighted to see them transformed into works of art. There are, however, many other places to look for clothes and remnants.

JUMBLE SALES
These sales are the most obvious source for rags, providing not only the cheapest but also the most eclectic selection of clothing. Here absolutely anything goes! A frilly, pink nighty or gaudy lurex dress could well be considered too tasteless to be sold in a charity shop, but no one would have any qualms about adding it to the pile at a jumble sale.

You'll soon learn to spot anything with potential at one glance, but just be prepared when your friends or neighbours see you carrying exotic and possibly embarrassing clothing! Be open-minded yourself; nearly everything has some kind of creative potential, and before you know it you'll find yourself getting excited about a woolly tea cosy, glittery socks or a pair of fluorescent surfer shorts.

CHILDREN'S CLOTHES STALLS
Children's stalls are often piled high with exuberantly colourful and bright cottons; look for toddlers' checked shirts, jolly socks and playsuits awash with an abstract boldness rarely found in adult clothing. Moreover, patterns and floral prints tend to be scaled down for little dresses, providing ideal proportions for most of the projects in this book. Children's T-shirts are also available in fine stripes of bold, irresistible colour combinations.

CHARITY SHOPS
Make a point of calling in to your local charity shop regularly; these establishments often have bags of rejects relegated to the back of the premises, and may be happy to pass them on for a small donation. They sometimes keep T-shirts to sell on by the sack to garages and antique restorers as soft polishing rags, and many a treasure can be found among them. While most adult clothing in charity shops is too expensive to cut or rip up, their children's section is often quite affordable.

ANTIQUE FAIRS AND MARKETS
Don't dismiss antique fairs and market stalls as too expensive to buy rags that you intend to cut or rip up. Certainly the cost of antique textiles is prohibitive, but damaged and stained embroideries, linens and laces, and 1940s crêpe hankies, scarves and dresses that are worn or damaged can often be bought cheaply. House auctions are another good source of older fabric.

Search for bold and interesting fabrics that catch your eye at sales and second-hand shops. A varied collection provides a good basic stock for all projects, and can help stimulate your design ideas.

DEPARTMENT STORES

Check the haberdashery departments and look through sale stock for fabric remnants and bundles of faded or unfashionably coloured ribbons or lace for dyeing. High-quality end-of-roll pieces are usually vastly reduced in price.

PROFESSIONAL ORGANIZATIONS

Contact theatrical costumiers to see if they will sell off anything that is beyond repair. I once bought a selection of satin ballet dresses in a delightful variety of colours because the net was badly worn.

Textile factories or warehouses, and even clothing wholesalers or dress-hire shops may have suitable pieces they would otherwise discard.

Samples of knitwear, from sweaters and old blankets to hats, waistcoats and socks, can be found in an abundance of patterns and colours, and can be put to excellent use in rag work.

MAKING INSPIRED CHOICES

Don't be limited to clothing when you are searching for materials to use; great inspiration can be found in other objects and even if they are not used they can remind you of a form, design or colour combination you want to imitate. Remember to look for lace, ribbons, bows, braids and other trimmings, as well as buttons and jewellery.

Pick up felt berets, feather-covered hats, 1950s floral decorated swimming caps and old straw bonnets, often with fabric flowers or a ribbon decoration. Sometimes you may only rescue a piece of soft net or lace, at other times your rewards can be bountiful and you may find thick sashes of velvet or crêpe flowers. Most essential of all is to pick out the jewel-like colours and exotic textures that excite you. If they sing out at you from a great heap of clothing now, they will invariably be just as inspiring to work with later.

WOOLS AND KNITS

While you are hunting for materials, keep your eyes open for knitted rags too: ski hats, scarves, gloves, leg warmers, tea cosies, even a decorative cuff or collar – in fact, any attractive piece of knitting that takes your fancy. Unfinished knitting projects, either your own or someone else's, can provide good woollen rags. The very vulnerability of knitting – its tendency to snag and become holey, to shrink, or for the style or colours to date – means that the likelihood of finding something special is pretty certain!

SHRUNKEN AND CHILDREN'S JUMPERS

So many beautifully knitted sweaters sadly make their way to the jumble sales as shrunken miniatures of their former glory. Fortunately, the felting that occurs when wool is boiled adds a firmness that makes the material easier to work in rag projects.

Children's sweaters and cardigans are also good finds. They can be made up into a special patchwork blanket in much the same way as children's dresses were traditionally cut up to make patchwork quilts.

PERUVIAN JUMPERS

These sweaters from the 1970s are full of rich pattern and intense jewel-like colours. Although they are too narrow for today's fashions, they can still be found at second-hand shops, market stalls and charity shops. Also look out for the soft brown-and-cream alpaca ponchos, hats and sweaters of the same period.

FAIR ISLE PATTERNS

Search for men's and children's Fair Isle pullovers and waistcoats. There always seems to be a similarity in the subdued colour blends used to make these beautiful patterns, which can probably be attributed to tradition, the fashions of the time and the limited availability of yarn colours. The joy of this is that a combination of assorted pieces of Fair Isle knitting invariably looks like the careful composition of many hours' work.

A friend once painstakingly knitted me a pair of gorgeous Fair Isle gloves in the most dazzling combination of shocking pink, ochres and Indian reds. My wretchedness at losing one was soon dissipated when I unashamedly cut up every part of the glove, including fingers, and stitched them into a random woollen patchwork blanket.

Children's and adults' socks with an attached leather sole have a folky charm and wonderful colouring which make them ideal to blend into patchwork. It is probably worth unpicking the sole in case there is more knitting underneath it.

PRINTED FABRIC

Small floral patterns, paisley prints, bright tartans and exuberant checks in natural fabrics are wonderfully inspiring, but do make sure that the fabric is printed on both sides. Faded bandanas are often found in a good selection of colours and can add a rustic freshness to projects.

Also seek out ethnic designs such as batik or indigo prints, leopardskin patterns or African textiles. If there is such a thing as the 'perfect garment' for rag art, the multicoloured Indian skirt comes close to winning the title: yards of hand-printed and dyed material, often with bands of harmonious variation in pattern and colour along the length of the skirt.

SILKS AND GLITTER

The dazzling textures of chiffon, lurex, satin or net are like the glitter of exotic jewels when they embellish a piece of rag work, whether it is a weaving, a rug wall hanging or a wreath. Easier to find amongst the rags than you would imagine, it is just a matter of tuning in to a certain textural look and feel.

Remember, too, that it is often 'odds' baskets that are full of little delights, such as fishnet and lurex tights in the brightest of pinks, tropical limes and oranges. The lure of a dress or blouse made of metallic shimmering fabric is irresistible and probably offers one of those rare occasions when you might splash out a bit. Moreover, a little really does go a long way, and it is something that can be used in many of the projects throughout the book.

Look for tiny floral prints, spots, tartans and stripes in clothing and fabric, but also choose larger patterns that have interesting colour tones.

SWIMSUITS

Out-of-date silky swimsuits have an intensity of colour that is not apparent in a lot of clothing. The combination of shiny fabric and vibrant summery colours is exciting to work with, and the fabric has the added bonus of not fraying.

LINGERIE

Sometimes the most unattractive of underwear or nightdresses can have useful elements, such as lace, frills, ribbon or broderie anglaise. Their very gaudiest aspects can make a stunning combination, such as lurid pink net from a waist slip with a lavender frill from a 'baby doll' nightie and, perhaps, deep blue fishnet stockings.

SCARVES AND TIES

Chiffon scarves, often with a few decorative threads of lurex, can be found in a multitude of shades. Try layering a few together to see the range of subtle colours you can create. At one time, head scarves were popular choices to give as gifts or holiday souvenirs, hence the great number found second-hand. In myriad textures, patterns and exotic colours, there is always a scarf suitable for cutting up!

Ties and cravats have a wonderful blend of silky texture and a perfect, small scale pattern. There is generally a handsomeness to the design that fits in well with ragwork. Paisley, striped or spotted strips cut from silk ties add a rich, enlivening vibrance to woven rag projects.

Glittery lurex, silks, net and lace, as well as such trimmings as velvet ribbons and decorative cord, will add sparkle and texture to rag work.

SORTING RAGS

A really large container such as a log basket is a useful item in which to keep your newly acquired rags until you are ready to sort them. Fabrics tend to pile up amazingly quickly, and you will soon find a need to prepare and organize them.

PREPARING RAGS

Cut off all seams, zips, hems and any other areas of clothing that won't be usable. Save buttons, lace, ribbon and embroidered trimmings. Pre-wash the remaining fabric, but don't worry too much about colours blending because it usually adds more interest! Tumble-dry the fabric or hang it on a clothes-horse. It will not be necessary to iron the rags.

SORTING BY TYPE

Now for the real pleasure of sorting through your dazzling collection of 'treasure'. Sort out all trimmings and keep them separately in boxes or jars.

Silks, satins and chiffons tend to be too slippery to stay firmly in place, so are not suitable for such projects as hooked rugs. Instead, save them in a separate basket to dip into when your work needs a bit of richness or to use for wall hangings or weaving. In general, all other types of fabrics can be mixed together.

SORTING BY COLOUR

You may like to sort your rags into colour groups, keeping russets and reds together, pinks and purples, blues and greens, and so on. Alternatively, simply gather a pile of fabrics in a big heap and see how they relate to each other. Make sure you have a large selection before you begin this process; it is so easy to make second-rate compromises if your choice is too limited at this stage. Gather together colourblends of rag that not only sit comfortably side by side, but also those that suggest a hint of richness, or set off a dormant sparkle or a shimmer in another fabric.

The basis of your colour choice can begin with a colour you've always been drawn to, or can perhaps be based on a hand-painted bowl, a vase of freshly picked flowers or just a simple postcard that attracts your eye. Perhaps you have been drawn solely to a blend of rusts, rich coral reds and umbers, and it is only when they are all placed together you realize that maybe your purple T-shirt proves just the accent needed to draw the whole look into something richer and more exciting.

The more you handle the fabrics and move colours around, the easier it will be for you to select and discard tones and textures. Place your final selections in neat, folded piles, then tie them together with strips of fabric.

STORING RAGS

Don't look upon your fabrics and trimmings as something to be kept out of sight. Appreciate the richness of colour and texture you have collected, and keep the fabrics attractively displayed as a constant inspiration around you. I have a favourite dark green basket that sits by the fireside, crammed with velvet, silks and cotton rags of earthy orange-reds, burnt sienna and rich terracottas. Unfortunately, it just looks too good to use!

There will be some fabrics in your collection that you do not foresee using for some time; these are best kept well-protected from light, moisture and dust in covered boxes or chests in a dry, dark location. In this case, you may like to include a moth-repellent sachet with your fabrics to keep them safe.

BASKETS AND BOXES

Simple cardboard boxes can be covered with beautiful paper or fabric. Particularly useful are boxes with lids for fabrics that you want to store for a longer period. Clearly label the boxes with the colours and types of fabrics or trims they contain to encourage you to reopen and explore them.

There are a huge number of second-hand baskets to be found in various shapes and sizes. Broken or weak handles can be strengthened by binding tightly with strong thread or raffia, and any basket looks more attractive once the handle is wrapped with fabric or ribbon. Wicker baskets can be painted with a light coat of gloss paint diluted with turpentine or white spirit, or simply sprayed with a car spray paint.

SHELVES AND CHESTS

If you have space in a workroom, or even a spare alcove, an alternative method of storage is to use a set of free-standing shelves for storing rags. This way you can see at a glance the range of fabrics from which to choose. Ideally, these shelves should be deep enough for a few baskets on the top to hold glittery rags, net and ribbon, and there should be enough of them to contain each colour range.

A chest of drawers or trunk is also a suitable place to store your materials, though you will find it less easy to organize and to see what you have. A better alternative is to use a special storage unit that has many individual drawers; some types allow you to label each drawer like a filing cabinet.

Folded fabrics, trimmings and remnants offer a wealth of decorative ideas at a glance when arranged in neat piles or in boxes and baskets.

CUTTING FABRICS

Most projects for ragwork require strips of fabric, which can be cut easily and continuously from a piece of fabric. This is fairly time-consuming, but is relaxing work to do and you may be able to persuade your family to help.

It is always a good idea to have a selection of ready-cut strips to hand, but if you have a special fabric and you are unsure what use you will put it to, resist the temptation to cut it up into strips.

Most fabrics can be cut with a good sharp pair of scissors, and any resulting fraying is all part of the honest charm of most rag work. For fabrics that fray easily, cut with a pair of pinking shears or on the bias, as described below.

If you intend to use the strips for hooking rag rugs, first hook a loop of a sample strip through some canvas with a crochet hook to check that it slips through comfortably, and is neither too tight, nor so loose that it slips undone. Once you are sure of the width that works for your project, you are ready for cutting.

CUTTING BIAS-CUT STRIPS

Fabric that frays badly, such as a special velvet or silk, is best cut on the bias (diagonally across the grain). Bias cutting is useful because the fabric has more flexibility, ideal when using rags for knitting or crocheting, and is less likely to fray. First, pull a short strip of the fabric to test that there is enough strength in the fabric before cutting a long length.

Follow the instructions for the second method of continuous cutting, but cut diagonally across the grain of the fabric (1). If you are unsure which way the grain runs, snip the fabric and pull a thread.

CONTINUOUS-CUTTING

The easiest method of cutting rag strips is to begin with a square or oblong piece of fabric and, starting at one corner, cut along the straight edge to a width of 1–2cm (³/₈–³/₄in), depending on the thickness of fabric. Keep this width from the outer edge, working toward the centre of the fabric (2).

The second method is to cut a strip across the square of fabric to the same width as above, but stop approximately 1cm (³/₈in) from the edge (3). Then start a new strip from the other direction. Keep cutting backwards and forwards along the material, never quite reaching the end each time so you achieve a continuous piece of fabric without breaks.

(2)

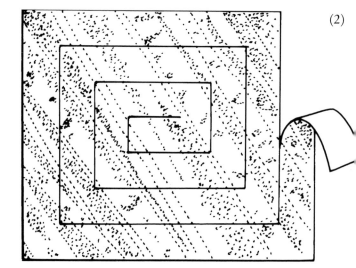

(3)

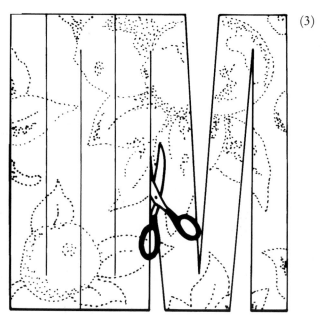

(1)

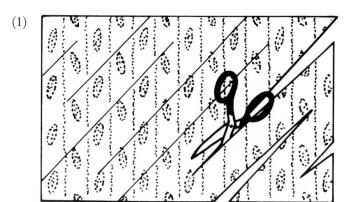

MAKING RAG BALLS

Ready-wound balls can be used for so many crafts, including knitting, crocheting, weaving, rag rugs and making seagrass stools. Rag balls can be stored in the same way as flat pieces of fabric (see page 15). Because of their size, they are easy to handle when sorting through and choosing colours for a project.

Wind the long rag strips into balls for easy, tangle-free storage. Simply coil an end of a strip and wrap the end round the coil in the same way as if you were making a ball of wool, frequently altering the direction. New strips can be tied or tacked onto the end of the previous strip. It is a very therapeutic and satisfying task to see your enormous pile of rags quickly transformed into inspiring and colourful rag balls.

Rag balls are a useful way of organizing fabric strips, and can be displayed in combinations of colours and patterns that inspire you.

Rag Rugs

There are two basic techniques for working rag rugs on a base fabric: hooked rugs are made by looping long rag strips through a base fabric or canvas, and prodded or 'proddy' rugs are made by poking little scraps of rag through hessian or fabric. Proddy rugs take considerably longer to complete and need to be worked on a frame. However, hooked rag rugs are ideal for beginners, and this method is emphasized throughout the chapter.

DESIGN INSPIRATION

Inspiration rarely appears out of nowhere: we all need to be fed continually with visual stimuli and it is not until you surround yourself with masses of colour, textiles, pictures and so on that you can begin to pick out the colours and images that instill some strong response in you and can lead to a design for a rug. There is no great skill involved in discovering what you like; it is just a matter of gathering enough strong and exciting images from which to draw ideas. Focus on the use of colours in combination with each other and compare how different shapes and patterns are arranged.

Begin by looking at the designs on ordinary items, such as a clothes-shop bag, perfume packaging, food labels, or the cover to a popular novel. Someone has spent a fortune on a team of designers to create an illustration that will have huge, instant appeal. You may well find that part of one of these, whether a colour blend, picture or pattern, is an element that can be used in a rag rug design.

PRINTED MATERIAL

Magazines have a wealth of striking images, especially in their advertisements. Headings to gardening, astrology or feature pages are sometimes accompanied by a piece of interesting artwork.

Promotional or calling cards sometimes have interesting and original ideas, photographs or even a piece of hand-painted artwork. Wrapping paper and greetings cards are also a joy to look through, especially the new and forever-changing designs. Postcards from museums, book shops or those sent to you from friends and relatives are also a good source.

FABRICS AND TEXTILES

Your collection of rags is immediately at hand, and you may find an interesting colour combination or pattern that would translate well to a rag rug. Also look for the work of modern textile designers. Their fabrics often have an abstract, painterly quality and their harmonious use of singing, vibrant colour is quite exhilarating. Buy small samples of any fabric designs that really excite you.

Indian and South American shops and market stalls have a stunning range of fabrics, ethnic embroidery, jewellery and folk art. Sometimes just a small purse can sow the seeds of a new project. The bustling atmosphere of flea markets is inspiring in itself, and you may leave with a bundle of tie-dyed clothes, or a broken basket that has some unique feature to copy into a design.

USING A SKETCHPAD

Take a sketchpad anywhere you go, to museums, cafés or park benches, so you can quickly jot down any designs or patterns you see. You will find that a certain amount is forgotten when you get home, and no matter what your drawing skills are like, your sketches and notes will be an invaluable prompt.

FILING VISUAL AIDS

Keep a folder or scrapbook to file postcards, newspaper or magazine cuttings or sketches. The folder could be decorated with a collage of pictures and materials that will induce you to pick it up frequently.

Find inspiration for your designs by taking a fresh look at the everyday items around you, or look at the work of craftspeople who you admire.

PLANNING A RUG DESIGN

When planning your design, consider whether you want to leave a border around your work and what width you want it to be. Rag rugs do not have to be square or oblong and you can make a circle, diamond, heart or any other shape.

Before making a sketch of your design, decide whether you are going to use hooked or proddy techniques, as this will affect your overall design to some extent; the proddy technique needs a simpler design than a hooked rug, as there will be less delineation.

SQUARE DESIGNS

The easiest designs are those based on a pattern of squares, such as the patchwork rug on pages 24–6. With this design, you need to divide the canvas into squares and choose colours to use. In fact, many types of canvas are already marked into 7.5cm (3in) squares. You could also create smaller squares inside larger ones, or create circles or hearts inside the squares for a more complicated design. Colour can be used to make a checked effect, or use stripes in each square or divide the squares by colour into triangles. This simple design has a lot of scope for adaptations.

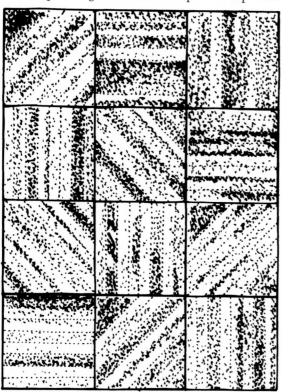

RANDOM DESIGNS

Not all rugs need meticulous planning. A sample I used for a demonstration was covered with colourful rags in odd L-shapes and lines, and created by various people who came along and tried their hand at hooking. This spontaneous, free-form method could just as easily develop in a pattern of random shapes.

ABSTRACT DESIGNS

A simple design such as a series of coloured shapes can be made with the cut-out process described below. Templates can be made of various shapes and simply arranged until a final design is created. More complicated patterns can also be designed this way, by using templates of flowers and leaves, for example.

TRANSFERRING A DESIGN

Once you have decided on your design, you can either draw the design freehand directly on the canvas or hessian. If you feel less confident, use cut-outs of shapes, or sketch a scale or a full-size drawing of the design. Transfer the design with a water-soluble felt-tip pen. Remember to leave a border around the base material when transferring the design.

USING CUT-OUT TEMPLATES

Trace shapes onto pieces of thick card and cut out to make templates. Round shapes can be easily traced from cups, plates and saucers. Move the shapes on the canvas until they form a pleasing arrangement.

Draw round the templates onto the base material. A little sketch of the design is useful, as the detail on the canvas won't be very strong and the sketch will remind you of the order if the templates move.

Left: A sketch of a patchwork square design has been made. A simple plan such as this does not need to be transferred to the canvas and just serves as a reminder of how to work each square.

Right: A rag rug that complements your room decor makes a real showpiece when hung on a wall.

SCALE DRAWINGS

Use graph paper with each square representing one or more canvas holes (this process is not suitable for a hessian or fabric base). Draw the design carefully on the graph paper, then repeat the design on the canvas, following square by square and noticing where the lines enter and leave each square. This method ensures that the critical shapes which need accuracy such as zig-zags are worked correctly by counting the holes.

FULL-SIZE DRAWINGS

You may find it easier to sketch a full-size drawing of the design, using the back of wallpaper or lining paper. This method is ideal for smaller rugs, and enables you to get a clearer idea of proportions and thus see how the pattern works on a larger scale. Either place the drawing under the canvas and draw the design on, or fold the sketch into eighths and trace section by section onto the base material.

BASIC EQUIPMENT

The basic materials for working a hooked rug are a rug canvas, a crochet hook and rag balls. If you want to devote a lot of time to this art form, or try the proddy technique described on page 27, there are other materials and tools you can use.

CANVAS AND BASE MATERIALS

Open-meshed rug canvas of strongly defined threads of 7mm (¼in) squares is available in a huge range of widths and gauges from craft suppliers and needle-craft specialists. It can be purchased starched, or unstarched for easier handling. This canvas keeps its shape and can be worked in the lap without a frame.

Hessian and sacking are the traditional base for hooking and prodding rags. Always buy the best quality, avoiding cheap upholstery hessian. Other evenweave fabrics could also be used. These fabrics will need to be stretched on a frame.

FRAMES

Artist's stretchers are already mitred and just need to be fitted together. Specialist frames with four pieces of wood, two of which have holes, have slits in the wood for inserting the base material. Rotating rug frames are also available.

HOOKS AND PRODDERS

Crochet hooks are used for hooking rugs on canvas, but can be hard on the hands. To customize the hook, wind a linen tape around the bottom for ease of handling. Turned wooden light pulls can often be found in craft shops with a central hole roughly the right size to hold a crochet hook; just wrap a few pieces of masking tape around the hook for a tight fit before gluing into the hole.

Special rug-making hooks with wooden handles are available from craft shops and have a slightly sharper hook than a crochet hook; these can be used on hessian or canvas.

Latch hooks are similar to wood-handled rug hooks with a deeper hook and a latch to allow wider pieces of fabric to be pulled through the canvas; these are only suitable to use with an open-mesh canvas.

Prodders with wooden handles can also be found in craft shops and these have just a point to poke the fabric through the base material. A wooden knitting needle makes a perfect substitute.

FINISHING AND BACKING RAG RUGS

Ready-made carpet binding is used for finishing off the edges of rugs on the back, and should tone with the colours of the finished rug. You can make your own binding by cutting a wide strip of fabric on the bias, long enough to follow the edge of the rug, and hemming the strip on the long sides before stitching in place. Binding should be pre-washed before it is sewn on. Follow the instructions for the Patchwork Hooked Rug on pages 24–6 for sewing on binding.

Use a lining fabric that is appropriate to the use of the rug for a backing; usually hessian or polyester is best. A backing is not necessary for rag rugs, and keeping the back open means you have easy access when it comes to carrying out any repairs.

BACKING A RUG

To back a rug, fold and secure the unworked canvas edges as described for the Patchwork Hooked Rug on pages 24–6. Then cut a piece of hessian, sacking, felt or strong linen fabric large enough to cover the rug canvas, allowing approximately 5cm (2in) extra all round to turn under.

Turn under a hem along the edges of the backing and press with an iron. Place right side up on the back of the rug and pin in place, making sure the backing joins the worked canvas along all edges. Slipstitch to the canvas with very strong thread.

Canvas or hessian, fabric strips and a crochet hook or knitting needle are all you need to make a rug, but if your enthusiasm grows, you may like to purchase more specialist equipment.

PATCHWORK HOOKED RUG

Hooked rugs involve making rows of looped fabric with a crochet hook or special rug-making hook. The technique can be used on open-mesh canvas or on a hessian or fabric base.

The border and squared divisions of the patchwork rug are all worked in the same colour, and the squares can be filled with any colour or design you like; the simple plan below was made to ensure that the series of stripes and diagonals were all lying in different directions to each other. As long as there is a common link of colours, it really won't matter how you work each one, and you can even decide on the pattern as you come to each square.

When hooking rugs, always begin and finish each fabric strip by working the end up to the front of the canvas, and trimming it to the height of the loops. Start a new strip in the same hole as the end of the previous rag strip to keep your work tight. Once you are at ease with the process, you can work in any direction you like.

This rug does not have a lined backing, but if you prefer to include one, follow the detailed instructions on page 23.

MATERIALS
- open-mesh canvas with 7mm (¹/₄in) threads, 60 × 45cm (24 × 18in) in size
- 2.5–3mm (size 2/0 or 3/0) crochet hook
- rag balls
- latex adhesive
- ready-made carpet binding

1 Use a water-soluble felt-tip pen to divide the canvas into 15cm (6in) squares, leaving a border of two or three holes around the outside. Transfer any design within the squares from the sketch to the canvas, as described on page 20.

2 Begin by working in one colour only. Use one row of rag for the border and for the squared divisions. With the right side of the canvas facing up, hold the crochet hook above the canvas and the end of the fabric strip underneath the canvas. Start at one corner and work along the edges first.

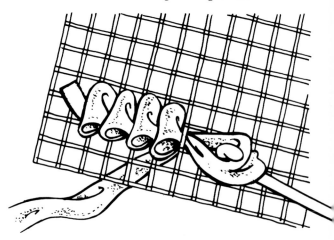

3 Push the hook through the first hole at a slight angle, catch the end of the strip with the hook and bring it through to the top, releasing the hook and leaving a small loop of fabric. Take the crochet hook through the previous hole, which is a border hole, and catch the very end of the strip, bringing it to the top; all strip ends need to be above the canvas.

4 Push the hook through the hole directly following the loop, catch more of the strip and bring it through the top. Repeat, working in a row along all edges. Then hook a row on the divisions between the squares. Make sure the loops are pulled through evenly and are all the same height.

5 To join new lengths of strips, finish the strip by pulling the end up through the next hole; then push the hook down through the same hole and bring up the end of the new strip.

6 Repeat the hooking process to fill all the squares, using different colours according to the design.

This patchwork rug uses a basic design of squares, which are then filled in with simple stripes in bold and striking colours.

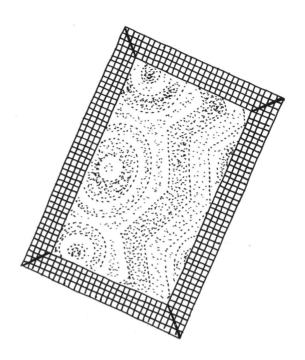

7 When the canvas is completely hooked, bring the last strip to the top of the canvas. Trim any long end strips to the height of the loops.

TIP
If the rug is positioned where it will be subjected to heavy use, cover the entire back with a thin layer of latex adhesive.

8 Now fold the border of unworked canvas under the edges of the rug. Turn the rug over and press down the border firmly. Glue to the back with latex adhesive or hand-stitch in place.

The striped pattern can be made rather randomly, by deciding on one, two or more rows to make up each stripe as you work.

9 Lay the carpet binding on top of the folded border so it meets the worked canvas at the edge, following the shape of the rug and mitring corners. Glue down with latex adhesive and leave to dry.

PRODDY RUG

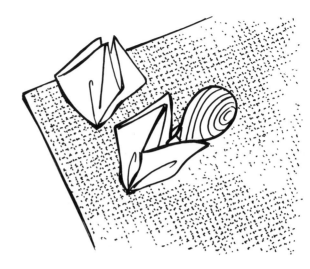

Proddy rugs are made by poking scraps or short strips of rag through a base fabric with a knitting needle or prodder; open-mesh canvas is not suitable because the fabric needs to be tightly packed.

The rags can be cut into any shapes – triangles, rectangles, squares or even circles. Each shape will create a different result, so it is best to practise with various shapes first on spare hessian to see what effect suits your design best.

MATERIALS
- hessian
- frame for stretching hessian
- rag squares, circles or other shapes
- prodder or wooden knitting needle
- latex adhesive

1 Cut the hessian to the desired size, transfer a design to the hessian (see page 20), and stretch the fabric on a frame.

3 Now push the prodder and fabric through the hole. Pull very slightly at the fabric on the back to make sure it is firm and gauge the amount that should stick out to make it secure.

4 Leaving a space of 2–3 threads between each hole, continue making holes and prodding fabric until the hessian is covered.

5 Turn the rug over and lightly dab latex adhesive on each fabric bobble. Finish the rug as described on page 23 or as for the Patchwork Hooked Rug.

2 Working from the first hole at one corner, make a hole in the hessian with the prodder. Fold a fabric shape in rough quarters and place the prodder into the folded centre of the shape, making sure the fabric is not pierced.

Coiled, Crocheted and
Knitted Rugs

Look beyond the cotton fabric traditionally used for rag rugs when choosing materials here:
consider using metallic threads, ribbons, or lace alone or in combination with fabric rags.
Coiled rope rugs can look special and elegant when made with satin ribbon, and a shimmer
of glittery or metallic fabric through a crocheted or knitted rug can make a unique work.
All these techniques can be worked on your lap, needing no elaborate frames.

DESIGN INSPIRATION

Look at examples of coiled rugs, baskets and pottery for ways to use pattern and colour in coiled rugs. Old plaited and coiled rugs, historically found in New England farmhouses, were often made from cotton fabric or a combination of cotton and wool. They frequently displayed a splendidly subtle contrast in hues because of the ever-changing strands and coils. Many beautiful African coiled basketry patterns, rich in symbolism, have been handed down from generation to generation. The coiled basketry of the North American Navajo Indian is also full of inspirational pattern work, and the designs can be transferred successfully to coiled rugs.

Various crochet and knitting stitches can also be studied to see how well they can be used with rag to achieve different effects. Commercial patterns are a great source for colour and composition ideas.

COILED ROPE RUGS

This form of rug-making is very similar in appearance to crocheted rag rugs, and ideal if you have difficulty with crocheting (see page 38–9). Rope rugs have a very neat and finished look, and are extremely strong and hard-wearing. The only drawback is the initial cost of the rope, and it is worth hunting around for an inexpensive source.

BASIC TECHNIQUES

The foundation of the rug is a coiled rope, and the rug can be worked in two ways.

For the first method (see Coiled and Bound Rug, page 30), a rope is secured in a coil with strips of fabric; this creates a textural and colourful appearance while binding the rope together into a firm structure. Because you see the results as you work, you can change colours of rag accordingly.

Hooking or prodding fabric strips are not the only method to making beautiful rugs from rags. Long strips can be wound round rope and coiled, or simply plaited or knitted into beautiful and surprisingly robust pieces.

Another method (see Wrapped-Rope Rug, page 33) entails binding the rope with rag, and then hand-stitching the fabric-covered rope into an evolving coil. Because the rope is bound first before coiling, you will have to make sure the colours of the fabric strips complement each other. Until the rug is completely coiled, the placement of colours will be unknown.

USING AND CHOOSING ROPE

The thickness of the rope will affect the rate at which your rug grows, so use thick rope if you want to create a very large rug quickly. To assess the length of rope needed for a rug, loosely wind the rope in a coil until you have reached the desired size; alternatively, work with a good supply and simply end and begin new rope lengths when required.

Ropes can be found from art and craft suppliers, or at DIY or hardware shops. Try experimenting with a variety of ropes until you find one that suits you; an amazing set of dinner mats can be made with the results of your tests!

Sash-cord rope, a natural and bio-degradable jute cord, is used for the following projects. This rope is thick, strong and has a firm structure.

Seagrass is less expensive than sash and has the required strength for rug-making, however it is thin and your work will grow at a slower rate.

Plied sisal has a firm, slightly bristly basis and could be used, but avoid unspun sisal as it is too loosely woven to be suitable.

Synthetic fibre ropes are often made into three-strand ropes in the same way as natural fibres; they have great strength and are damp-proof.

CHOOSING FABRIC

It is possible to use a broad variety of materials; slippery satins and silks are especially good choices because they are held firmly in place.

Try using materials and colours in combination, too. Ribbon, old scarves and ties provide a strong textural contrast with flowered and checked cottons. Lace or net layered over fine fabric enlivens a poorly textured area and creates a spattering of exciting undertones. The variation in colour tones of tie-dyed and marbled fabrics are also shown to advantage in coiled rugs.

COILED AND *BOUND* RUG

The beauty of this rug is that there is no need to plan the size of your rug in advance; simply work until you reach the desired size, then finish. Make sure the rag strips do not twist as you work, so the fabric lies evenly on the coil.

MATERIALS
- 2–4 packets of 12.5m (41ft) sash cord or other rope
- strong thread
- blunt, large-eyed tapestry needle
- assortment of fabric strips
- dry glue stick

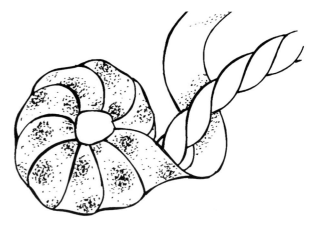

3 Gluing the end of the strip to the back of the coil, take the strip up through the centre of the coil, over the front and wrap round the back. Continue wrapping the strip through the centre of the coil, until the coil is filled with rag.

4 Now wrap the strip round the loose end of the rope only. Then wrap the strip round the loose end and into the centre of the coil to secure the rope to the coil. Continue alternating these 'short' and 'long' stitches, coiling the rope round, until a full circle has been made.

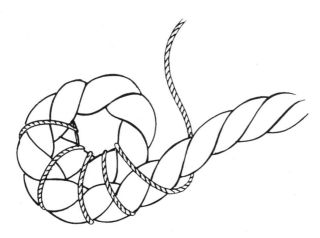

1 Cut the end of the rope at a shallow diagonal angle, and bind it tightly with strong sewing thread to make it thin and to prevent fraying. Wind this end into a small coil and bind tightly with thread, working from the centre outwards.

2 Cut a workable strip of fabric, and thread through the blunt, large-eyed needle. If the fabric will not go through the eye, wind clear adhesive tape tightly around the strip to create the firm effect of a needle.

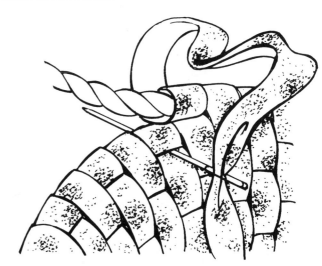

5 For the next row, wrap the loose rope in a short stitch as before, then take the long stitch into the previous row rather than the centre. Continue

The finished coiled rug makes a unique feature in a room, particularly on a hardwood floor.

working round the coil, but whenever the fabric starts to slope backwards instead of radiating evenly from the centre, increase the stitches by working two stitches into the space instead of one.

6 To join a new fabric strip, cut the old strip just behind your last long stitch on the back of the coil, and lightly glue the new piece on top. Work the stitch round several times in the same space to reinforce the join.

When selecting new strips of fabric to work into the rug, choose according to how the colours are blending as you work, to avoid a concentration of one colour in any particular area.

7 To finish, cut the rope at an angle as in step 1, so it sits smoothly and tightly against the outside edge of the rug. Glue the remaining strip firmly round the tapered end. Cut the strip and secure to the back by stitching neatly in place.

8 If a small hole remains at the centre of the rug, create a decorative finishing touch by sewing on a button that is covered in a striking or embroidered fabric.

TIP
To join new lengths of rope to the rug, taper the old and new uncovered ropes as in step 1, stitching the two tapered ends together neatly.

WRAPPED-ROPE RUG

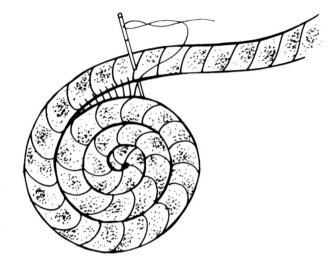

The simple circle design created by the bound rope is a more simplified version of the Coiled Bound Rug and ideal for the beginner, though the rug is just as robust and durable.

MATERIALS
- sash cord or other rope
- needle and strong thread
- dry glue stick
- rag balls in assorted colours

1 Taper one end of the rope and bind with stitches as described in step 1 of the Coiled and Bound Rug.

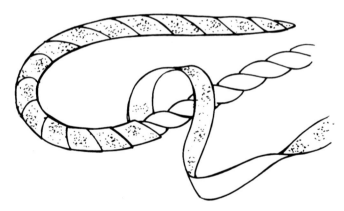

2 Glue one end of a fabric strip to the tapered end of rope and wrap round the rope, bandage style. Apply more glue as necessary to keep the fabric in place, and join a new fabric strip by gluing it to the old strip.

3 Then wind the tapered end into a small coil. Stitch the fabric-wrapped rope together with a few firm stitches. Then continue stitching the coil, taking a little fabric from each side and working round in a spiral.

4 When the end of the rope is reached, taper the rope, as in the first step, and wrap the remaining fabric strip round, gluing the fabric to secure. Neatly stitch the wrapped tapered end to the edge of the rug.

TIP
To join new lengths of fabric-wrapped rope, end the rope as in step 4 and begin a new rope in the same way, making sure the two tapered ends fit together neatly round the coil.

Plaiting a Circular Rug

A plaited or braided rug has a traditional, home-made charm that looks just right in any setting, whether by the bed, on the hearth or cosily nestled near the kitchen range. Fabric plaiting can be used to produce rugs of almost any shape, such as oval, rectangular or circular. Most types of sturdy fabric can be used, but a smoother, less amateur effect is created if the fabrics are kept to the same weight.

You can work directly from rag balls, folding the strip in half lengthways as you plait. Alternatively, cut wider strips, about 3cm (1¹/₂in) or so wide, then press along a lengthways fold.

MATERIALS
- long fabric strips
- safety pins, needles and strong thread

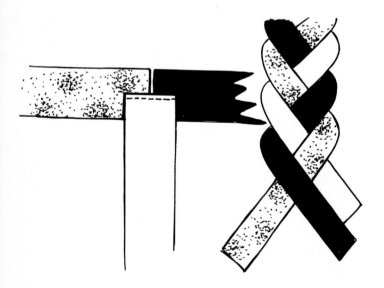

1 Place the three strips in a T-bar, as shown; then pin and stitch together.

2 Using a large safety pin, attach the joined strips to a chair back or a hook.

3 Plait by taking the right strip over the middle length, then bringing the left strip over the new middle length, and continue. Keep a firm and even tension, making sure the fabric strips lie so the open side of the fold is always on the right; this raw edge will be hidden to the inside of the rug when the plait is coiled. Pin the end of the plait to secure.

4 Working on a flat surface, insert a strong, knotted thread into one end of the plait. Run the thread through the bottom loop of the next plait, stitching it back to the starting point and pulling tight. Catch the next few lower loops, bringing each stitch back to the centre to create a firm coil.

5 To continue, keep working round in a spiral, but stitch the plait together by catching a little fabric on the inside edges of each row. Do not pull the thread too tightly or the work will pucker.

Alternatively, tie a length of thin cord to the thread and lace from side to side between the loops, not penetrating the fabric.

6 Continue until the rug is the desired size. To join new plaits, simply sew on three new fabric strips and plait before stitching round the coil.

7 To finish the rug, trim the three strips into a taper. Plait the tapered end and secure with stitching. Sew into the edge of the rug.

Plaited rugs are so simple to make and give the room a homely charm. Rectangular or oval rugs are other options you may like to explore.

RECTANGULAR RUGS

Make a plait to the desired length of your rug. Repeat, making as many plaits as you want the width of the rug to be. Stitch the plaits together, side by side, leaving the ends free as if fringed.

Alternatively, create a rectangle as you plait. Begin with several plaits, then make a corner by bringing the left strip over the centre strip three times, then carrying the right strip over the centre and pulling it tight. Keep making corners around the edges and adapt the length of the straight plaiting to the desired shape of the rectangle. When the plaiting is completed, the rug is in position and ready to be stitched.

CIRCULAR-WORKED RUGS

Begin a circular rug by plaiting your left strip over the centre strip twice, then the right strip tightly over the centre; keep repeating this until you have a circle about 5–6cm (2–2¼in) in diameter, and then plait in the normal way. When the desired size is reached, stitch the plait together.

OVAL RUGS

First, plait a straight strip to the length of the centre of your rug. Then curve the end as for a circular-worked rug, above, plaiting the left strip over the centre strip twice and then the right strip tightly over the centre. Continue plaiting down towards the other end of the centre plait and create another curve. Carry on plaiting in the conventional way, and finish by stitching the plait together.

You can either sew the plait in a coil by taking a little fabric from each side, as here, or for a stronger effect, lace cord through the loops to join the plait into a coil.

KNITTING A RAG RUG

Knitting with rag is an exciting alternative to wool. Treat the balls of fabric as your yarn, and use fairly thick needles; begin with 6.5mm needles until you find a size suitable for the thickness of your rag.

Knitting patchwork squares that are then sewn together is the easiest way to handle bulky rag. Very large rugs can be knitted using this method, and you will avoid a huge number of stitches on your needles and an unwieldy bulk of work on your lap. The key to linking them is the blending of colours; for example, try a simple series of stripes in different sizes stitched together in a variety of directions.

The rug can be finished with a knitted, crocheted or plaited border in a toning or contrasting colour.

KNITTING A SQUARE

Ideally, use a stretch fabric, such as old T-shirts, stockings or rags cut on the bias, because the fabric's flexibility makes knitting easier on your hands. Knitted T-shirt rags are the most practical of all fabrics, especially for bathroom rugs, as they won't fray, lose their shape or unravel with heavy use and constant washing.

MATERIALS
- rag balls
- 6.5mm knitting needles

1 Cast on 15–20 stitches, depending on the size of square desired.

2 Knit in stocking stitch until a square is formed; from time to time stop and measure the piece to ensure the square is finished on the correct row.

3 Cast off on a knit row. Repeat, making as many squares as needed for the desired size of rug, then sew together.

CROCHETED RUGS

Crocheted rugs are one of the most pleasurable forms of rug-making. The rug can be worked on your lap and grows at a rapid rate. It costs nothing in materials beyond the price of a large crochet hook.

The rag rug is worked using rounds of double crochet stitch from a simple base of five chain stitches. If you are new to crochet, practise the stitches below with yarn first, then using rag strips, until you are comfortable with the craft and find it effortless.

BASIC CHAIN STITCH

Using a large crochet hook, secure a piece of rag to the hook with a slip knot. To do this, make a loop at one end of a rag strip, right over left, insert the hook into the loop, catch the right-hand end and bring through the loop to the front, pulling to tighten the knot; the knot should be loose enough to easily slip along the hook.

Now bring the long rag strip under and over the hook from back to front, hooking and drawing it through the loop on the hook. Repeat this action until the chains are evenly sized and neither too loose nor too tight.

DOUBLE CROCHET STITCH

Insert the hook into the second chain stitch from the hook, from front to back. Hook the strip and draw through the chain. Bring the long rag strip under and over the hook, and draw the strip through both loops on the hook. For the second row, insert the hook under both loops of each chain stitch.

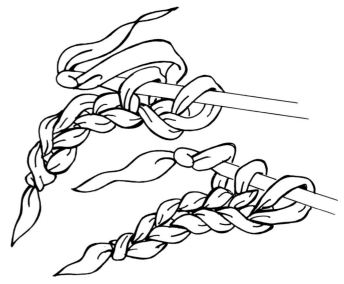

CROCHETING A RUG

This type of rug-making does use up a lot of rag balls, so make sure you have a good supply in blending colours before starting your work.

MATERIALS
- rag balls
- large crochet hook

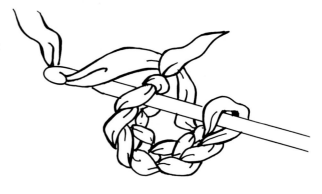

1 Attach a long rag strip to the crochet hook with a slip knot and work five chain stitches. Hook the first stitch onto the crochet hook, and join the two ends with another stitch through both loops to make a ring.

2 For the second row, work eight double crochet stitches into the ring as described opposite, working round in a circle.

3 Increase the number of stitches in the third row by working twice into each stitch. For the fourth row, increase every alternate stitch. Assess the best time to increase the stitches as rows are worked – as soon as the sides begin to gather up, it is time to increase the stitches.

This multicoloured rug is made with a double crochet stitch. Although you may find the rag bulky to work with at first, the results are astounding.

4 To finish, cut the end of the rag strip, leaving enough to darn in. Bring the strip end under and over the hook and draw it through the last loop on the hook, pulling tightly. Tuck the loose end underneath the rug and stitch neatly in place.

Weaving with Fabric

A great textural and colour range can be achieved by weaving with all types of fabrics, ribbons, lace, cellophane and any trims you may have. Weaving is actually a very uncomplicated process, accomplished by weaving a weft (widthways) thread over and under a warp (lengthways) thread. Wall hangings, framed pictures, throw-rugs and cushions are just some of the projects you can create.

TYPES OF LOOMS

Weavers in earlier civilizations produced beautiful textiles from a minimum of basic equipment. One of the earliest methods, still used today, is backstrap weaving in which the warp threads are stretched between two sticks or pieces of bamboo; additional sticks are inserted to help the weft through. The loom is simply hung on a branch or door handle and pulled tight by the weaver to whom another loom strap is

attached. The North American Navajo Indians used a similar two-strap loom to weave beautiful blankets and textiles.

In primary schools, a child's first introduction to weaving is often a cardboard loom. My interest in rag weaving first came about after my thirteen-year-old daughter, disappointed at the progress of a school weaving project, made a simple cardboard loom, grabbed my basket of rag balls and proceeded to weave the most delightful piece of work in about ten minutes. Weaving on card looms involves no cost, an absolute minimum of craft skills, and is an ideal opportunity to use some of the more exuberant colours and wild textures.

CHOOSING MATERIALS FOR WEAVING

Gather together the most exciting materials you can find, such as net, chiffon, ribbon, lace, velvet, lurex, small vivid patterns, tartans and spotted prints. If you are making a wall hanging from the weaving, you can choose even wilder materials such as cellophane, foil and colourful plastic bags. To add sparkle to a piece, glue on gemstones or dabs of glitter glue after weaving is completed.

FRAMING WEAVING

Small pieces of weaving are best displayed as framed pictures. To do this, first paint an old picture frame to tone in with the colours of the weaving. Make sure the inside measurement of the frame is considerably smaller than your finished piece of weaving.

Cut cardboard to the size of the inside frame, cover it in a generous layer of dry glue stick, and stretch the weaving over it, pressing it down firmly and smoothly over the edges. Catchstitch the edges of the weaving to the back of the card at each corner to hold it firm. Slip the work into the frame and hold it in place with a few fine panel pins, masking tape or brown sticky paper.

Samples of rag-weaving, however small, can be made up into objects to admire. Frame smaller pieces for eye-catching pictures full of colour and texture, or make up larger ones into multicoloured cushions and wall hangings.

MAKING A CARDBOARD SHUTTLE AND LOOM

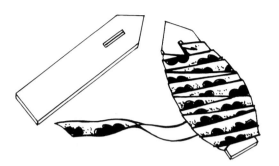

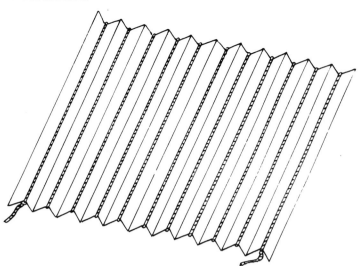

Cut a strong piece of card or cardboard to a square or rectangle, depending on the shape you want for your finished piece. Then cut simple, parallel v-shaped notches top and bottom, ready to take the warp threads. Before you begin cutting, spend a few minutes drawing a series of straight lines along the length of the card to ensure your notches line up and are equally spaced. The notches do not need to be as close as in conventional weaving.

Thread the loom with any firm yarn that comes to hand. Begin by looping yarn between the first two notches top and bottom on one side of the loom and tying them in a knot on the back; then wind the yarn firmly through the notches until you reach the other side, knotting on the back to secure. Rag strips are then woven back and forth across the width of the loom.

To make a shuttle, cut a point into one end of a strong card strip, then cut a slit into this end. Thread one end of a rag strip through the slit and wind the remaining rag round the shuttle.

WOVEN WALL HANGINGS

Large pieces of weaving look beautiful displayed on a wall, but the edges will need to be attractively finished. Make a feature of the ends by fashioning a knotted fringe. Cut and knot the warp ends after weaving, but keep the ends a reasonable length.

Starting close to the weaving, wrap wool round a small group of the threads, trapping the end of the wool. Continue winding the wool round until you have a tassel. Then pull the end of the wool under and to the top of your wrapping with a fine crochet hook.

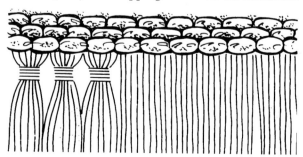

WOVEN CUSHIONS

The vibrant colours and textures weaving produces are put to good effect in cushions. This project uses one long piece of weaving, which is then folded and sewn to create a 22.5cm (9in) square cushion with weaving front and back. However, you could also use a small weaving and back it with fabric.

MATERIALS
- cardboard loom, measuring 27.5 × 50cm (11 × 20in)
- firm yarn for the warp thread
- card shuttle, about 2.5 × 17.5cm (1 × 7in)
- net, chiffon, lace, ribbon, wool, lurex, colourful tights and Indian scarves, cut into strips
- cushion pad or wadding

1 Thread one end of a rag strip into the shuttle and wind the rest of the strip round the card.

2 Thread the loom with firm yarn, as described on page 42. Starting on the left and working right, weave the rag over and under the warp threads. Turn the shuttle at the end of the row and weave back to the left side, changing the under-and-over sequence. Gently push down the new row of rag weaving against the previous row.

3 Continue weaving rows until the loom is full. Join new strips by leaving the old strip hanging loose at the end of a completed row; then re-thread the shuttle and begin a new row.

4 Turn over the loom and cut through the warp threads on the back. Knot the loose ends of the warp threads into pairs along the top and bottom and trim; then fold to the back of the weaving and neatly stitch out of sight. Trim and stitch any loose weft ends to the back.

5 Now machine topstitch the front edge of each side so the edges are firm and solid.

6 Fold the weaving in half widthways with the wrong side out. Hand-sew or machine stitch around the edges, leaving a gap for stuffing. Clip the corners, then turn the cover right side out and insert the cushion pad or wadding. Turn under the raw edges and slip stitch the gap closed.

Although bright pieces of weaving make stunning cushions, you may like to choose more subdued shades of fabric, depending on your decor.

43

WOVEN STOOL

Weaving raffia and jute for stools is perhaps not the popular hobby it once was, but by binding the seagrass with strips of colourful and patterned fabric, the process is revitalized into an inspiring and contemporary craft. The finished stool takes on a richly and decorative texture that leaves the original looking drab and unexciting alongside it.

Although the woven stool looks quite complex, once the initial weaving pattern and rhythm is established, it is simple and relaxing to work. A stool can be completed easily in one session, although binding the seagrass can be time-consuming. Stools with rectangular seats or any square-framed chairs can be worked in the same way with slight modifications.

New wooden stool frames and seagrass can be purchased from most craft suppliers, but second-hand shops, jumble sales and household auctions are excellent sources for original stools. They often cost very little and are available in a wonderful variety of shapes and sizes. The very small, low, square-shaped stools are perfect for your first attempt at weaving.

Look, too, for suitable chair frames. Many chairs with rush seating are simply discarded because they are costly and time-consuming to repair, so can often be found second-hand.

PREPARATION

Strip off the old seagrass by simply cutting through with a sharp knife. Trying to salvage and re-use the original material really isn't worth the trouble; it makes the process of stripping very lengthy and the material is often too dirty to work with. Clean the stripped framework, pull out any odd nails, repair loose joints and treat for woodworm, if necessary.

If you want to paint or stain your stool to tone in with your fabrics, do so well before weaving so the paint has a chance to dry completely. Old pieces of furniture are sometimes highly varnished and may need thorough sanding or an application of white spirit or methylated spirits to get back to the natural wood. Painted stools in good condition will just need sanding to remove any loose paintwork and create a smooth surface.

Use a primer undercoat to paint the stool or chair. The paint is oil-based, very hardwearing and has a matt finish that looks effective with rag-woven seats. The range of colours is a little limited, but they can be customized with the addition of a few artists' oil colours. Drab green, for example, can be transformed into a wonderfully rich dark green with the addition of Hooker's green, burnt umber and a touch of black. Don't squirt the paint straight into the pot: experiment with a small quantity in a separate dish before mixing up a sufficient amount to cover your stool.

When the undercoat is completely dry, additional paint effects can be applied. More interest can be added to a plain painted surface by lightly sponging on a muted colour, such as diluted raw umber, with a natural sea sponge.

A chair and stool frame have been woven with a combination of rich, colourful fabrics to create a set which will brighten any corner.

COVERING THE STOOL

Avoid bulky fabrics, and try to keep to similar weight cottons for an even finish. If you are cutting fabric especially for the stool, the strips can be a little wider than the standard 1-2cm ($^3/_8$-$^3/_4$in), and this will help speed up the binding process (see page 16). Select your colours first, making sure they will all work together in any combination, and try to find an even balance of plain, checked and floral fabrics so the pattern will be varied.

MATERIALS
- rectangular wooden stool base
- 1kg (2lb) pack of seagrass
- strong card to make a shuttle
- dry glue stick
- plenty of rag balls

1 Cut off a manageable length of seagrass and wrap a strip of rag around it, bandage fashion, gluing the beginning and end of each strip securely in order to fasten it (see Wrapped-Rope Rug, page 33). The more frequently you change your fabric, the more colourful the effect will be. Continue until all the seagrass is covered.

If you are weaving a larger stool or chair, increase the amount of seagrass you need. It is better to have too much covered now than to run out of your supply when you are weaving.

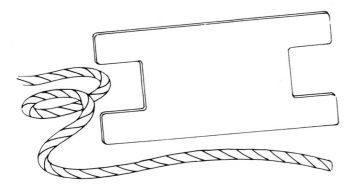

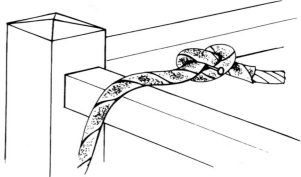

2 Make a shuttle from the card. To do this, cut a card measuring 20x10cm (8x4in). Cut out a notch on each side of the short ends, about 2.5cm (1in) in from the corner edges and to a depth of 4cm (1$^1/_2$in). Wind your wrapped seagrass around the shuttle or into rag balls (see page 16).

3 Knot the end of a length of wrapped seagrass and nail the knot to the inside of the left-hand bar, 2.5cm (1in) from the inside front bar. Pull the strip tightly over the front bar, keeping it against the corner; carry it underneath and pull it through the inside. Wind it over the left bar, pulling it back to the inside.

The vibrant colours and rich textures of rag weaving transform an old stool and provide it with a completely new lease of life.

5 Keep this simple pattern going around the stool, always making sure that the strips are tight and butt up next to each other. Constantly pulling the seagrass tightly can be hard on your hands and you might like to wear soft gloves.

Take care that the lines cross each other at right angles, and check the underside to make sure that the seagrass isn't twisted or going diagonally across the corner. The more neatly and firmly the stool is worked, the harder it will wear and the better it will look.

6 To join new lengths, remove the fabric off the end of the old strip and one end of the new strip. Tie the two ends together with a reef knot. Make sure the join falls underneath the stool and can be tucked away neatly. If it does not, remove more fabric from the finished strip to enable the knot to be tied further back.

7 To keep the tension, try to finish weaving the stool without stopping. If you do have to stop, tie the end tightly around the leg a few times. You will find as you progress that the shorter sides will be completely filled first, well before the longer ones. To finish off, just work to and fro between the longer sides in a kind of elongated figure-of-eight until the centre hole is filled.

8 When the rectangular stool is completely filled with woven fabric, secure the last strip underneath the stool with a figure-of-eight knot. The layered weaving will give the finished stool tremendous strength.

TIP
Square stools are worked slightly differently as the sides will fill up evenly with woven fabric. Near the centre, it will become difficult to use a shuttle or ball of fabric. To finish off, simply push a single length of seagrass in and out until the centre is filled.

Chairs can be narrower at the back, so you will need to compensate for this by taking occasional extra turns over the front bar until the shape is even.

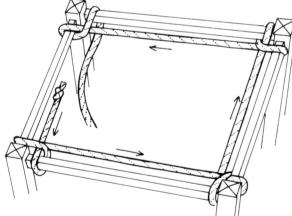

4 Take the strip along the front bar, over the right-hand side bar, and under as before. Then take it over the right-hand corner of the front bar and under. Repeat on the remaining two corners.

Decorative Room Furnishings

Colourful rags and motifs cut out from fabric can be used to decorate any room in the house; curtain poles and rings can be bound with rag strips, furniture can be embellished with glued-on fabric motifs, and walls can be adorned with a combination of fabric motifs and stencilling effects. When deciding which fabrics to use, carefully consider your existing room decor. Antique fabrics have a subdued elegance that blends well with wood, but more contemporary fabrics have a vibrance of colour perfect for a child's room.

CHOOSING FABRICS

When selecting fabrics for room furnishings, remember that the finished effect should enhance, not overwhelm, the setting; you will probably need to hold your fabrics up to the walls or drape them over chairs in the room to see how well they blend in with the interior decoration. Extra fabric from any soft furnishings such as quilts or duvet covers, cushions, curtains or upholstery are excellent sources and will help tie the whole look together. However, be cautious with your choices – you do not want the room scheme to be too over-coordinated.

When choosing fabrics for cutting out motifs, it is important to ensure the motifs can stand on their own and that they don't intertwine or overlap into other areas of the design. Old 1930s and '40s tablecloths and cushions often have lovely floral motifs that can be cut out; there is an original charm and elegance to some of these old fabrics that enables them to transfer very successfully to wall and furniture decorations. More contemporary fabrics may also have useful designs, and highly patterned stripes and borders are perfect for making into wall borders or for edging cupboards and chests.

USING FABRIC MOTIFS

Although there are many fabric images you may like to use for decorating, floral motifs are the most popular, and leaves and tendrils blend easily together with flower heads. Because the fabric should blend into the background of your furniture or wall, avoid very bulky fabrics.

When cutting out motifs, first roughly cut round the detail you want; this will allow you to hold the fabric piece easily in your hand while cutting out intricate areas. Use a pair of small, pointed scissors to snip into corners and round curves. Try to choose motifs that have some interesting, feathery edges; this will give more subtlety to the finished design.

Adding decorative rag and stencil work to home furnishings, such as walls, curtains, furniture, or even lampshades and cupboards, enables you to give rooms your own individual style.

CURTAIN POLES AND RINGS

Plain wooden curtain rings and a pole can make a beautiful multicoloured set when bound with rag. The simplicity of the decorated pole and rings has a rather rustic, folky effect that makes a charming feature in a room. Choose any fabrics that suit the room or curtains you intend to hang. Two large and two small rings were covered with rag and wedged on the ends of the pole to create decorative stops. You may prefer to use more rings to create thicker finials.

If you prefer not to wrap the pole, paint it instead. Acrylics are quick-drying, but you could use any paint you like, such as emulsion, undercoat or gloss. Use colours that tie in well with the colour and design of your fabric-wrapped curtain rings. You may like to paint the pole a solid colour first, then pick up the curtain ring colours by painting alternate circles of colour round the pole. If you decide to do this, mask off areas you do not want to re-paint. Simply stick masking tape down in rings round the pole; by using different widths of tape, you can create thick and thin stripes.

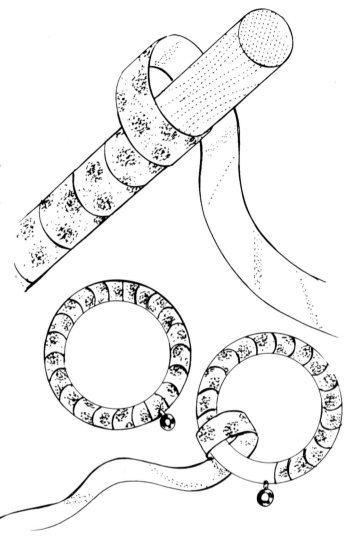

MATERIALS
- old pine curtain pole, broomstick or length of dowelling
- set of large plastic or wooden curtain rings for hanging the curtain
- 2 small and 2 medium plastic or wooden curtain rings
- acrylic paints in colour to tone with fabric
- dry glue stick
- balls of rag
- cold glaze or spray varnish

1 Make an inexpensive curtain pole from a broomstick, or from a length of dowelling if a longer one is needed. Alternatively, buy an inexpensive, plain pine pole.

2 Glue the beginning of a rag strip firmly to one end of the pole using a generous amount of dry glue stick. Wind the rag round the pole, bandage fashion, until completely covered.

When a crooked zig-zag in the strip is reached (an effect of continuous cutting, see page 16), cut through the zig-zag and rejoin the strip with dry glue stick. Join new lengths of rag in the same way. When completely covered, paint the exposed ends with acrylics and leave to dry.

3 Now cover the curtain rings. Dab dry glue stick on one end of a rag strip and bind round a curtain ring in the same way as for the pole, securing the end with more dry glue stick. Repeat the binding process for all the rings.

4 Seal the pole and curtain rings with cold glaze or spray varnish and leave to dry.

5 When the rings and pole are dry, slide the covered curtain rings on the pole, retaining the two medium and two small rings to use as stoppers or finials at the ends. Then push one large fabric-covered ring on the end of the pole, followed by one small ring; repeat at the other end of the pole. The decorated pole is now ready to hang curtains.

The bold colours of rag-bound curtain rings and pole gives liveliness to a room, and a border of fabric sewn onto the curtain adds the final touch.

TIP

For added effect, use a plain-coloured curtain and sew a hemmed border of the rag fabric along the inside length of each curtain to coordinate with the curtain rings and pole.

DECORATED FURNITURE

I discovered the possibilities of decorating furniture with fabric after falling in love with an imitation wood-grain chest-of-drawers in a soft warm yellow, decorated with the simplest of hand-painted roses. The chest-of-drawers sold at an exorbitant price at auction, so I made do with a slightly damaged, satin walnut set of drawers, which I decorated with a wavy paint effect and glued-on floral fabric cut-outs.

Similar, plain oak chest-of-drawers are often available from junk shops, and are perfect for decorating with fabric. Other pieces of furniture can also be decorated this way, such as bureaux, dressing tables or occasional tables. Chairs with a circular seat make an ideal surface for decoration, and fabric motifs can be arranged in intricate designs.

BASIC MATERIALS

You will need a comb for the wavy paint effect; this can be a plastic Afro comb, or you can make your own. To make a comb, cut a rectangle from a strong piece of card or a plastic lid and cut equally spaced long pointed prongs from one end of the card or lid, making sure the prongs are wider than the gaps between them.

DECORATING A CHEST-OF-DRAWERS

For this project, you will need firm fabric of soft chintz roses, muted hydrangeas or other floral designs that have motifs which are easy to cut out. If the floral fabric does not include leaves and tendrils, cut out a variety of leaves from another fabric that will compliment the flowers and look natural.

MATERIALS
- chest-of-drawers
- fine and coarse sandpaper and wood block
- newspapers or plastic sheeting
- paintbrush
- cream undercoat
- white spirit
- polyurethane satin varnish
- yellow ochre and raw umber artists' oil colours
- Afro comb, or cardboard or plastic hand-made comb
- waterproof marker pen and ruler
- floral fabric
- dry glue stick or mapping pins

1 Sand the chest-of-drawers to create a flat, even surface on which to paint. Wrap a strip of coarse sandpaper around a small block of wood to give even pressure, and sand in the direction of the grain. Repeat, using fine sandpaper to achieve a smooth finish.

2 Lay newspapers or plastic sheeting under the chest to protect surfaces from paint. Remove the drawers from the chest and stand them on end for ease of painting.

3 Mix yellow ochre with the cream undercoat until a warm, earthy, cream colour is created. Paint the chest and fronts of drawers evenly with the creamy paint. Leave to dry.

Delicate fabric floral motifs are artfully arranged on the chair and chest of drawers to make a pretty bedroom duo. This method of decorating furniture allows for ornate and elaborate designs, and is similar to découpage.

4 Mix a quantity of satin varnish, slightly diluted with white spirit, with yellow ochre and raw umber oil paint to make a tinted glaze; reserve some of the satin varnish for a final coat.

Paint each part of the chest separately with the glaze, creating a wood-graining pattern by combing a wavy line through the glaze with the comb while the glaze is still wet. Repeat on the fronts of the drawers. Leave to dry.

5 When the varnish is completely dry, sand again lightly with fine sandpaper. Define the shapes of the drawers by drawing lines round the edges using a ruler and waterproof marker pen.

6 Cut out the flowers from the fabric. Place them in various positions on the drawers and top surface of the chest to see where they look best; secure them with a tiny dab of dry glue stick or a mapping pin. Then cover the back of each motif evenly with dry glue, and stick them in position.

7 Dilute the reserved varnish with white spirit and paint one coat on the chest and drawers, making sure the absorbent fabric areas are well coated.

8 When dry, sand with fine sandpaper. Repeat the varnishing and sanding process until all the surfaces feel smooth and the fabric flowers blend in well.

The round seat of a chair is the perfect space on which to create a garland of floral motifs, and the wide expanse of the chair back can echo the design.

FABRIC AND STENCIL WALL BORDERS

Decorated borders on walls, around windows or above or below a dado or picture rail, adds interest to interior decoration, and the use of fabric allows you to match your wall decoration to existing soft furnishings. By combining motifs cut from a dominant fabric in a room such as a bedspread or curtains, with stencil effects, the blend of paint and fabric prevents the result from looking too overworked.

The inspiration for this project came from a pair of curtains that had been included in a lot from an auction. Although these odd, unwanted curtains were faded along the sides and worn with age, the floral motifs in the centre were still extraordinarily rich, with deep undertones of colour and a perfect design.

I had rather amateurishly stencilled roses under a stained-glass window in a room, and decided to overlay the stencilling with cut-out flowers from the curtains; this new decoration not only obliterated the stencilled roses, but brought new life to a dull area and a richness that could never have been equalled by a conventional wallpaper border. The motifs were cut from a fairly bulky linen and stuck to the wall with dry glue stick, and the leaves were then stencilled around the motifs. Although floral motifs have been used here, simple abstract shapes and ethnic designs can blend sympathetically with dragged and colour-washed walls.

USING STENCIL TEMPLATES

You can use the template provided for the leaves, or a ready-made stencil purchased from an art and craft supplier. To use the template shown, simply slide it under acetate film or clear plastic and trace the design with a marker pen, leaving a deep border around the

You can easily make your own stencil using the trace off pattern given overleaf, or trace your own from a fabric motif.

edges. Then cut out the areas you want to paint with a scalpel. The transparency of the stencil enables you to register it accurately onto the fabric design.

The template can be easily reduced or enlarged on a photocopier to suit your requirements. You may like to adapt the design to suit the layout of your decoration by moving the template under the film or plastic until a different arrangement of leaves is created, tracing each leaf independently.

DECORATING A WALL

When stencilling, apply the paint as dryly as possible; a second coat can be applied if the colour is not dense enough. After each application, check the back of the stencil to make sure no paint has seeped through to the other side.

MATERIALS
- cut-out floral fabric motifs
- dry glue stick
- acetate film or stencil plastic
- fine marker pen
- sharp craft knife or scalpel and cutting mat
- low-tack masking tape
- stencil brush
- acrylic paint, poster or gouache in green colours
- spray varnish

1 Prepare the wall for decoration, making sure it is clean, grease-free and dry. Then arrange the motifs along a border of the wall, sticking them lightly down with glue stick and rearranging them until the desired composition is achieved. Leave spaces around the flowers to add stencilled leaves.

2 Coat the back of each fabric motif with more glue stick and place in the final positions.

3 Enlarge or reduce the leaf templates first, if you wish, then trace them onto acetate film or clear plastic using a fine marker pen.

4 Place the film or plastic on a cutting mat, right side up, and cut out the design with a craft knife. Work on one area at a time and keep the knife fairly upright. Gently move the stencil, rather than the knife, round awkward curves.

5 Position the stencil on the wall and either hold it in place or lightly tape it down with masking tape. Dip the brush into the paint and dab off the excess onto a scrap of paper. Apply the paint using a firm dabbing action, filling in the cut-out area of the stencil. Stencil as many leaves as desired around the fabric floral motifs.

6 While the paint is still wet, try blending in another shade of green for more depth of colour. Leave to dry.

7 When dry, spray the whole area with varnish.

The colours and floral design used in this wall border echo those of the stained-glass window. Plan the positioning of the motifs and stencils carefully to maximize impact.

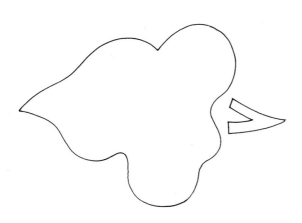 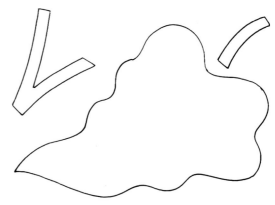 

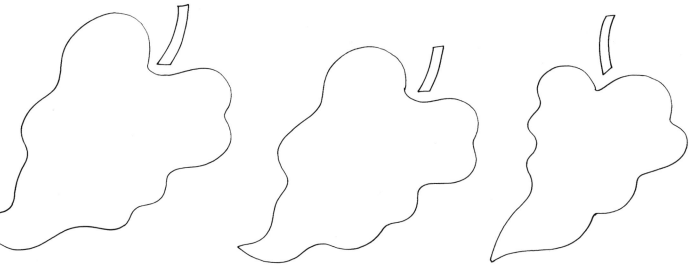

Greetings Cards

Making your own fabric greetings cards requires little skill or cost, and is a very individual way to send a personal message. Fabric collages, patchworks and motifs can be glued onto cards, or just a beautiful textile square can be mounted. Small pieces of hooked rag rug can also be made into interesting and highly textural cards. Whether you are designing one or mass-producing a quantity of cards, you will find fabric an inspiring medium for a range of different visual effects.

DESIGN APPROACHES

Greetings cards can be designed as an ordered composition that requires some thought and advance planning, or created using simple or more random methods. The easiest technique is to glue a square fragment of an attractive textile in a mount or to the front of a hand-made card.

You can vary this approach by cutting out one or several motifs from fabric and mounting these on card. Taking this idea further, you can create a random collage of overlapping motifs and scraps or even a patchwork of fabrics pieced together into a design.

For more ordered compositions, look at the paintings and collages of various artists for your inspiration. Search through the racks of art postcards in stationery or card shops, and pick out the work of well-known painters. Or, look in galleries, art books or special exhibitions. Don't be daunted by the notion of looking around antique fairs at expensive Art Deco china, textiles and jewellery. The ideas you see can be quick to jot down, involving just a few simple sketches and should be graphic and simple enough to cut out of fabric.

CHOOSING FABRICS

When acquiring and cutting up so many colourful rags, it is easy to lose sight of the design aspect of slightly larger abstract and floral motifs. Some of this bold imagery can be captured by carefully cutting the motifs out and using them in various combinations. Worn textiles or thick furnishing fabrics are good choices for cards consisting of a single fabric square.

Look for beautiful 1920s and '30s fabrics depicting the tulip, daffodil and nasturtium. Also very effective are small pieces of *toile de jouy* (single-coloured fabrics depicting highly detailed pictorial scenes), kitsch images from the 1950s and bold ethnic abstract textiles. The Art Nouveau-inspired designs of intertwined poppies and lilies, the natural images of William Morris designs and Victorian chintz roses of every size translate well into greetings cards.

Crêpe handkerchiefs from the '30s and '40s, though inclined to be a little worn around the edges, are often full of the most handsome colours and designs, and have a delightful period appeal to them. And amongst the heap of rags you have gathered, you may have found some interesting designers' labels; some have a hand-painted effect which is worthy of mounting.

Try decorating a piece of colourful felt from an old beret with beads, buttons and tiny scraps of fabric. And if you try the marbling, sponging or printing techniques on pages 114–19, you might like to frame samples of these as cards.

With beautiful fabrics, simple card mounts in various colours and just a little time, you can create a superb range of greetings cards.

MOUNTING DESIGNS

To complete the projects on the following pages, you will need some sort of mount or card base for your decoration. The easiest, but most costly, option is to use ready-made mounts which are often conveniently sold with envelopes.

Alternatively, you can create your own mounts – either just a plain card or a card with a cut-out window. If you decide to do this, you will first need to buy the envelopes and some large pieces of card for the mounts in a colour of your choice. As it is difficult to find a correctly sized envelope to fit a previously made card, you will need to cut the cards to fit the envelopes.

USING READY-MADE MOUNTS

Plain-coloured blank cards can be bought ready cut and framed in a variety of shapes, sizes and colours from needlework, art and craft suppliers. They are ideal for mounting small pieces of special fabric; for example, the embroidered cuff from an Indian dress, a detail from a knitted tea cosy or a piece from a rich tartan kilt. Thick pieces of fabric such as these can simply be lightly glued with a latex adhesive so they sit neatly within their mount; finer materials such as silk scarves or ties will need to be plumped out with a little wadding before gluing into place.

MAKING A MOUNT

A plain card makes a simple mount, but a more professional result is produced by cutting 'windows' into the card, and squares or rectangles are the easiest shapes to cut out.

MATERIALS
- envelopes in the colour of your choice
- pieces of card in the colour of your choice
- ruler and pencil
- cutting mat, scalpel or craft knife, and metal ruler

Making card mounts, with or without windows, is easy to do. Choose a colour of card that works well with your fabric piece, providing a good strong 'frame' without overpowering the fabric.

1 Measure the envelope and make a simple card template slightly smaller all round. Insert the template into the envelope to make sure it fits in easily and comfortably. This will be the finished card size.

2 Double this measurement and cut out pieces from the card to this size, then fold in half to make a plain card mount. Alternatively, lightly pencil round the template twice onto a large piece of card, cut out and fold along the edge where the two drawings join. Leave the cards plain and glue a decoration to the front, or cut windows from the card.

3 To cut a square window, lightly pencil a square on the inside of the front of the card, making sure the square is centred. Place the card on a cutting mat and, using a craft knife or scalpel against a metal ruler, cut out the square in smooth movements. To make a bevelled edge, angle the scalpel at about 60°.

4 Once the window is cut, the decoration can be taped down to the inside front of the card. If desired, cut another piece of card to the size of the template and glue this on the back of the decoration to make a neat finish.

ABSTRACT CARDS

This project uses the colourful, and painterly discs of Sonia Delaunay as the basis for the design, but you may prefer to adapt this method using the work of any other abstract artist you find inspiring. The paper cuts of Matisse consist of simple, loose collections of colourful shapes that can easily be reproduced with fabric scraps. Or just looking at the works of such artists as Picasso, Klee and Mondrian may give you a starting point for your design.

USING A TEMPLATE

Trace round the bases of cups and coins onto card and cut out to make templates. Place the templates on the wrong side of pressed fabric, trace round with a water-soluble pen or pencil, and cut out the shapes. Using templates will ensure that your circles are completely round.

MATERIALS
- variety of fairly firm fabric scraps in cotton, felt, satin and silks
- ready-made mounts
- card
- latex adhesive or dry glue stick

1 Cut the card slightly larger all round than the window in the ready-made mount.

2 Using card templates as described above, cut circles of different sizes and colours from fabric.

3 Arrange the circles on the card in a series of overlapping patterns, cutting some in half and changing them around until an interesting design has developed. When arranging, remember that the edge of the card will be hidden inside the mount.

4 Glue the circles in place, beginning with the ones at the bottom first and building up the layers.

5 When dry, insert the finished card into the mount, gluing it in place round the edges to secure.

FABRIC POSTCARDS AND PINBOARD

These cards are designed so they all look attractive as a group when displayed together on a pinboard. Of course, you do not need to show them off in this way, but the idea of a linked design means that they can be used as invitations or for other occasions when you want to present a special theme.

Your cards could represent a particular era, by using a rich mixture of fabric pieces from 1930s silk scarves, crêpe handkerchiefs and dresses, for example, or by choosing bold, abstract floral and fruit prints from '50s aprons. You could create a simple colour theme to tone with a room setting; set a certain style, such as ethnic, floral, abstract or country; or just group an eclectic collection of fabrics you find exciting.

A collection of striking and original cards would make a very special gift. An eighteenth birthday present could contain pieces of material from personal items such as old baby clothes, a special piece of embroidery or fabrics reminiscent of the recipient's style of dressing, and could then be displayed on a small framed pinboard or packaged in a special box.

MAKING THE POSTCARDS
This is a splendid way of using up small pieces of special fabrics such as an embroidered skirt border or a scrap of antique clothing.

MATERIALS
- blank postcards
- special pieces of fabric
- dry glue stick
- latex adhesive for thicker materials such as embroidery
- sheet of acetate or stiff clear plastic
- marker pen

1 First, make a transparent, postcard-sized template. Place an old postcard onto a piece of acetate or clear plastic and draw around it with a thick marker pen. A thick pen is needed to clearly define the border. Cut around the outline. Using the template will ensure that the exact part of the pattern is cut out.

2 Place the template on the fabric, moving it around until you find the ideal position, then roughly cut around the template.

3 Cover the front of a blank postcard with the glue stick; it is essential that it is covered evenly as air bubbles could ruin the finished effect.

4 Gently place the fabric on the card, pressing carefully and pushing out any air bubbles until perfectly smooth. Turn it over and trim the extra fabric away so it lines up neatly with the postcard edges. Allow to dry, and repeat the process for as many cards as required to fill the pinboard.

DECORATING A PINBOARD
To fill up an entire pinboard with a series of thematic postcards would be a fairly costly exercise, and certainly not as personal and intriguing as a set of images you have created yourself.

Pinboards can be purchased fairly cheaply and decorated by painting the cork with acrylic paints or emulsion to tone with your choice of fabric colours. The frame can be painted in a complementary colour or by using a sponged, distressed or other paint effect. When you have painted your pinboard and it is dry, simply pin the fabric postcards onto it in an attractive arrangement.

If you intend to use a number of pinboards, you could make your own. Old picture frames without glass are usually inexpensive, and can be filled with thin insulation board cut to size. Working from the back, lightly pin the board into place and tape to the frame using masking tape or brown sticky paper.

The deep red of the pinboard sets off the designs of the fabric postcards. The pinboard instantly enlivens a room at little cost and provides a constant reminder of the beauty of fabric.

COLLAGE CARDS

The joy of these cards is that they can appear in-dividual and hand-made, even though they are in fact produced in large batches. They are created by mak-ing a large collage that is then cut into pieces, and this technique is the perfect way to use up the tiniest of lovely fabric scraps as well as ribbons, trims, and even decorative paper motifs.

A good time to work on the cards is just after Christmas while you are still surrounded by festive spirit and inspiration. It is a splendid activity for the whole family as it doesn't matter if a number of peo-ple work on the collage; the more spontaneity and ideas that are put into the work, the more fabulous it will turn out. Any ribbons, lace, netting or fabrics left over from Christmas can be reused in the collage, and the cards can be used for thank-you notes.

First you will need to buy the envelopes and some large pieces of card for the mounts in any colour of your choice. This project uses black card to set off the colours of the fabric. The amount of thick sheets you will need for your collages depends on the quantity of cards you are making, and you will need to estimate this roughly.

The decorative centre can be any size you desire within the card mount. A small piece can look strik-ingly effective when mounted on a plain expanse of blank card. Or you may prefer to leave hardly any border at all.

MATERIALS
- envelopes and black (or other colour) card for mounts
- large sheet of thick card for the collage
- dry glue stick or latex adhesive
- fabric scraps, ribbons, trims and decorative paper cut-outs
- gold glitter glue or gold acrylic paint

1 Measure an envelope and make a simple card template slightly smaller all around than the envelope. Follow the instructions on page 60 for making your own mounts.

2 Now decide on the design and size of decoration for each card. If the fabric decoration is to fill the card, the decoration will need to measure about 1cm ($^3/_8$in) less all around than the template. Make the border wider for large cards than for small ones.

3 To make the collage, completely cover the large thick sheet of card by gluing on an assortment of fabrics, trims and cut-out motifs. Start off by covering the entire sheet in large pieces of fabric to fill in the background and gradually build up a more detailed piece of work.

Any size of scraps can be used. Tiny decorations take longer to glue down, but the intricate detail that results means that the collage can be cut into smaller pieces. Overlapping edges can be trimmed when the collage is complete.

4 When the sheet of card is completely covered in fabric scraps, turn it over. Divide the back into equal sections with a pencil and ruler, according to the dimensions of the pieces required.

5 Cut out the individual collages carefully. Turn them over. Carefully look over the pieces. There may be a few weak areas that could benefit from a little brightening up: a few squirts of glitter glue or gold acrylic paint will soon bring them to life.

6 Finally, glue the individual collages to the mounts, pressing them down firmly.

TIP
You may prefer to insert your collage designs in ready-made card mounts as a quicker alternative.

Beautiful and original collage cards are easy to produce in quantity. Use this technique for Christmas cards or special invitations when you need to send out lots of cards at once.

Decorative Wreaths and Rings

Wreaths, crowns and garlands have been a traditional method of celebrating in many cultures, from the laurel wreaths worn by the Romans to the wreaths and rings celebrating the autumn harvest, Easter and Christmas. Using rag to create sumptuous wreaths gives this traditional craft a new twist and allows a greater freedom with colour and texture than by using purely natural materials.

WREATH BASES

Wreaths can be purchased from many sources, including florist suppliers, craft shops, basket importers and gift shops. They vary widely in the materials they are made from, which include cane, twisted vines, straw and grass. The tightness of the weave of the ring will decide to an extent how you are going to work your rag. Loose cane will mean you can pull loops of fabric through the spaces with a crochet hook, whereas a tight weave will probably necessitate tying strips of rag around the whole thickness of the ring.

Alternatively, you can create your own wreath. To do this, intertwine the stems from a climbing plant such as a honeysuckle or vine, fashion them in a circle and hold the ring together with twine. Brittle or dry stems can be made more flexible by soaking in warm water. Keep winding the stems around in this circle until it is thick and firm. Before adding decoration you will need to leave the wreath in an airing cupboard or other warm, well-ventilated area to dry.

DESIGN INSPIRATION

The inspiration for wreath design can come from any source, such as a special holiday or celebration, a time period, a colour scheme or can just be dictated by the trimmings you have in your collection. The memories of a special trip can be rekindled by decorating a ring with, for example, textured rag and fabric fruits to suggest the exotic colours of a tropical holiday. Driftwood and shells can be accompanied by fabrics of muted ochres and blues to hint at the understated tones of the seaside, and little mementos such as coins, pebbles or tickets can be subtly tied onto a ring to blend in amongst the evocative textures.

You may like to create a special celebratory golden wedding anniversary gift by covering a wreath with small ties of gold ribbon, lurex strips, lace, net, beads and clusters of chains. Try spraying net and lace with gold paint, and add drops of glitter glue to create a jewel-like effect on strips of cellophane. Re-use any golden gift ties and cracker wrappings, and make use of sparkling jewellery and odd earrings.

Using similar methods, a simple colour theme can be the basis of a rag-decorated wreath, either to blend in with and soften the effect of the rich, deep colours in any room, or to accentuate them. Fabrics, lace and ribbons can be dyed to create a collection of tonal variations that would be difficult to find anywhere, and the addition of beads, buttons and odd pieces of jewellery can enrich it with texture and depth.

The style of wreath you make can be as varied as the materials you have at hand. Along with fabrics and trimmings, you will need a wreath base, and these are available in a range of sizes.

Seaside Wreath

This ring was inspired by a seaside holiday. The muted yellows and the cerulean and ultramarine blues in the surroundings captured my imagination.

My children were young, and evocative images of them in flowery pink T-shirts and spotted shorts are preserved for me by the little fabric scraps kept from their worn-out clothing and hair ribbons.

The materials listed below are, of course, arbitrary: the choice of fabrics, colours and textures will very much depend on your own personal experiences.

The base for the seaside wreath consists of a fairly thick, rustic canework ring, and small areas were deliberately left exposed to reproduce the effect of smooth, curved driftwood. There is no formality about the ring; it is purely a soft, decorative representation of the memories of a family holiday.

MATERIALS
- cane wreath base
- crochet hook
- toning pieces of felt, chiffon, ribbon and wool
- assorted scraps of cotton fabric
- wadding or cotton wool
- buttons or beads
- driftwood, shells, stones, coins or souvenirs
- needle and thread
- odd pieces of jewellery

1 Cut strips from the felt, chiffon, wool and cotton, making sure the strips are long enough to pull through the cane wreath and knot. Reserve some cotton fabric or a special fabric that you want to highlight to use for making the padded balls.

2 Using a crochet hook, pull small strips of rag gently through the spaces created by the cane ring; hold them in place with a simple knot. Cover the ring entirely with the fabric strips, ribbons and cord, varying the texture as you go.

3 Now make the padded balls. These add softness and texture to the design and can be any size you like; however, large balls will overwhelm the wreath. Cut a circle of fabric and stitch an even running stitch round the edge. Place a piece of cotton wool or wadding in the centre.

4 Draw up the stitching in a gather and hold it in place with several stitches, then take a stitch right through the centre to create a little indentation in the ball. Make a selection of balls and stitch them together in groups of two or three. Run strong thread through the back to tie them to the wreath.

5 Tie the clusters of balls onto the wreath, so they are equally spaced.

6 Tie on the driftwood, shells, pebbles or pieces of jewellery, and stitch on toning buttons or beads. Driftwood, shells or stones and coin tokens often have small holes; if they do not, you may be able to bore a little hole carefully with an awl. Add a fabric loop at the top for hanging, if desired.

A jumble of trinkets, cord, ribbons and shells is cleverly arranged to make an enchanting wreath that is evocative of the seaside.

LARGE RING OF HEARTS

This huge ring has an extravagant amount of rich decoration and is a wonderful compilation of ideas found in this book. It is enriched with rags and ribbons, padded clusters, fabric-covered beads and eggs, painted buttons and masses of colourful fabric hearts.

Tartan and small-patterned cotton fabrics are perfect for hearts that are going to be stitched with a sewing machine, and this is the best way to produce a large amount quickly. Felt hearts are also included on this wreath, and are easily and decoratively stitched together by hand.

MATERIALS

- large, round cane or vine wreath base
- cotton fabrics in small prints and tartans
- felt in complementary colours
- card for making a template
- tiny beads and buttons for decorating the hearts
- embroidery silk in various colours
- cotton wool or wadding for stuffing
- hand-painted or fabric-covered buttons (see pages 94–5)
- fabric-covered polystyrene eggs made with silk or crêpe (see page 84)
- dry glue stick
- fabric-covered wooden beads (see page 77)
- odd pieces of jewellery
- rag strips, ribbon, cord and lace
- padded balls (see page 68)
- tassel and cord

1 Trace the heart template onto a piece of card and cut it out. Use the card to cut heart shapes from printed fabric and felt.

2 Decorate half the hearts with beads, jewellery, buttons, tiny scraps of felt or embroidery stitches.

3 To make a fabric heart, sew two heart shapes together with wrong sides facing, allowing a gap for stuffing. Turn right sides out and stuff evenly with cotton wool or wadding. Turn under the raw edges of the gap and slipstitch to close. Run a length of embroidery silk through the top or back of the heart to make a tie. Repeat to sew all the hearts together.

4 For a felt heart, simply hand-stitch two felt cut-out hearts together with a running stitch, leaving a gap, then stuff with cotton wool or wadding. Close up the gap by continuing the running stitch.

To create a charming, naive feature, use colourful embroidery silk for the stitches or add a blanket stitch or cross stitch round the edges. Thread a length of embroidery silk through the felt hearts using the same method as for the fabric ones.

5 Tie the fabric and felt hearts all over the ring so they are evenly distributed. Fill in spaces by tying on strips of rag, ribbon, lace and felt, trimming them so they do not overshadow the hearts. Use the scraps of felt left over from cutting hearts to tie through the cane for intense bursts of colour and texture.

The profusion of hand-decorated felt hearts, broken up with tiny felt shapes and baubles, makes a wreath that is full of texture and detail.

6 Tie clusters of fabric-covered beads onto the ring to break up the rich textures of the hearts. Add old jewellery to weak-looking areas.

7 Thread the covered eggs with embroidery silk (see page 85 for threading). Attach them to the top of the ring, leaving a gap between them.

8 Plait three strips of fabric, stitch into a coil, and sew on the wreath between the two eggs.

9 To make the centrepiece, tie a tassel to a length of cord, then thread on fabric-covered wooden beads. Tie the tasselled cord to the top centre of the wreath so it hangs between the eggs.

MULTICOLOURED KNIT WREATH

This little heart-shaped wreath was decorated using a pair of child's knitted, leather-soled socks; the soles were carefully unpicked so that every scrap of the colourful and delightfully patterned woollen socks could be used. The surface is decorated with small woollen disks, coils of yarn and tiny woollen balls.

MATERIALS
- wreath base of any shape, but not too thick
- multicoloured knitted woollen pieces of various sizes
- textured yarns in blending colours

1 Cut strips from knitted garments, wide enough to encircle the wreath and leaving enough spare to fold the edges under in case of fraying. Stitch each strip together on the back of the wreath. Continue stitching on strips until the wreath is covered.

2 Now make the woollen discs. Cut a small circle of knit, fold the edges under, with the raw edges tucked in, and stitch to secure; a touch of latex adhesive on the back will remedy fraying. Repeat the process to make as many discs as required.

3 Stitch the discs onto the wreath, either singly or in clusters.

4 Stitch coils of yarn scraps and pieces of unravelled knitting lightly onto the wreath.

5 Now make a cluster of tiny balls to place at the top of the heart. Fold small pieces of closely knitted scraps, stitching them on the back to secure. Then decorate the balls with French knots made with wool. Sew these balls in a cluster to the apex of the heart. Add a ribbon or fabric loop for hanging.

These two wreaths, though quite different, show how small, bright scraps of fabric and knitwear can be built up into an exciting combination of texture and colour.

HEART-DUO WREATH

This idea is worked round two heart-shaped wreaths, one small enough to fit inside the other. It would work equally well with two circular shapes. The inner shape is bound with silk and the outer one is packed with dozens of tied scraps of rag and ribbon, and decorated with beads, buttons and odd pieces of jewellery.

MATERIALS
- two cane wreath bases, one fitting inside the other
- long silk scarf or fabric for the inner wreath
- strips of felt and rag
- scraps of ribbon, wool, cord, embroidery silk and lace
- odd earrings, brooches, buttons and beads
- needle and thread

1 Bind the inner, smaller wreath with a band of bright silk that blends with the rags and decorations. To do this, attach the beginning of the strip to the back of the wreath with a small stitch, and bind it round the heart wreath until it is completely covered. Secure the end to the back with a few stitches. Now place to one side.

2 Work the larger wreath by hooking lengths of rag and felt through the spaces between the cane and tying them into single knots. Organize the tying so the knots are placed evenly over the front and sides of the wreath, leaving areas of cane revealed between each tie. Leave the inner area of the wreath free of decoration so that the smaller heart can fit comfortably inside it.

3 Tie pieces of wool, ribbon, embroidery silk, cord and lace in between the rag strips to fill in any empty spaces round the wreath.

4 Stitch buttons onto the centre of the ties. Thread beads, odd earrings and old broken brooches with embroidery yarn and attach them to the cane with several knots and a decorative bow.

5 Now place the smaller wreath inside the outer one; if it doesn't fit tightly, link the two with a few strands of fine ribbon so that these lie over the inner heart, blending the two wreaths together. Add a loop of ribbon for hanging, if desired.

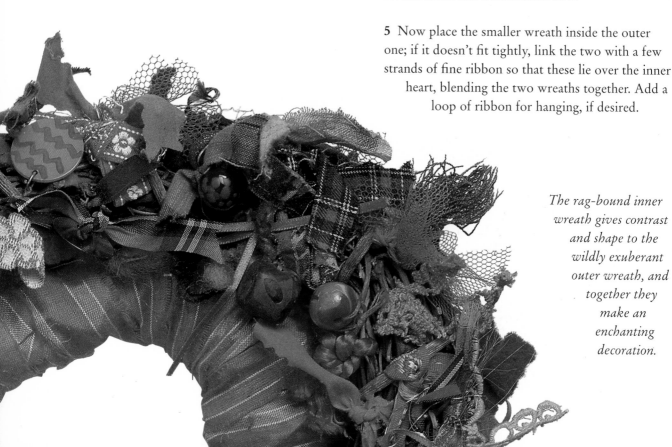

The rag-bound inner wreath gives contrast and shape to the wildly exuberant outer wreath, and together they make an enchanting decoration.

WREATH OF SOFT SCARVES

This soft heart-shaped wreath relies on the gentle fall of crêpe and silk scarves and handkerchiefs for its slightly sensuous impression. The fine stitching on strips cut from the edges acts as a delicate weighting when the pieces are tied.

Several 1930s handkerchiefs of glowing reds and yellows were the inspiration for this particular wreath, and led to a search for silk scarves, cravats, spotty chiffon headscarves, old crêpe dresses and matching net. Some very old crêpe materials may fade in bright sunlight, so be careful in your choice of place to display the finished wreath.

The method of attaching the fabrics to the wreath is very simple and quick, but do allow plenty of time for the selection and cutting of the materials. The wreath's finished effect is completely dependent on the colour blends and choice of materials.

Gather a piece of the fabric in your hand to see how effective it looks in terms of the design, how it fits in with your other pieces, and the intensity of colour created if it is folded several times. This will also help you decide how wide the fabric should be cut.

MATERIALS
- heart-shaped wreath base
- assortment of crêpe, silk and chiffon scarves
- crêpe handkerchiefs
- pieces of net and ribbon

1 Cut strips from the fabric along the length of the hemmed edges to keep the finely stitched line.

2 Now tie each strip around the wreath so the knots are tied in different places, making sure that there is an even distribution of bulk. Make use of the finished edges as much as possible. The ties should hang softly into the centre to keep the shape of the heart, and the colours should blend in a soft variation around the wreath.

3 Finally, tie small net and chiffon bows round the outer edge to help fill in any sparse areas. A simple ribbon can be added at the top to hang the wreath.

The soft folds of chiffon and crêpe hang to the centre of this wreath, giving it a fluidity and prettiness.

Luminous shiny fabrics, exotic colours and the rich texture of grape clusters and net give this wreath a sparkling splendour.

TROPICAL WREATH

This tropical wreath was inspired by a desire to brighten up the kitchen one dark winter's day. Multi-textures are created by using clusters of fabric balls, suggesting the lush fruits of the tropics. The grapes are made from a mauve T-shirt and wooden beads.

MATERIALS
- thick, round wreath base
- satin or silk swimsuits
- lace, net and chiffon scarves and socks
- floral prints
- children's striped T-shirts
- mauve tie-dyed T-shirt
- cotton wool or wadding
- wooden or polystyrene beads

1 Cut the fabric into strips, reserving the mauve T-shirt and some fabric for making padded balls. Cover the wreath completely in tied-on rag strips, staggering them so that both the front and sides are evenly covered in rag bows, ties and knots. Try to vary the texture and colour distribution.

2 Make some padded balls from fabric (see page 68). Vary the textures, using satin, velvet, flowered cottons and dyed lace. Decorate the centres with beads, buttons, frills of ribbon or net bows. String the balls into clusters and tie them on the wreath.

3 Next, make the grape clusters. Cut the mauve T-shirt fabric into circles, stretch each circle round a bead and bind at the top with sewing thread. Link them together in a grape-like formation with a few firm stitches. Tie onto the wreath.

4 Finish by attaching a ribbon or fabric loop for hanging, if desired.

CHRISTMAS WREATH

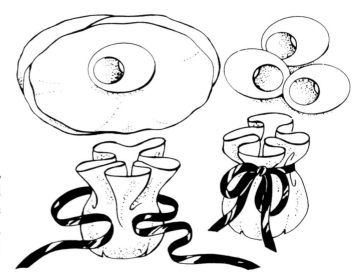

Although the wreath looks complex in construction, it is, in fact, a simple structure consisting of a round cane base and a small plastic bracelet. The wreath has been worked in vivid shades of red, green and gold, but softer colours of green and white, perhaps blended with hessian, would work equally well.

MATERIALS
- cane wreath base
- plastic bracelet
- small wooden or polystyrene beads
- metallic fabrics and braids, such as lurex or gold lamé
- tartan and Christmas fabrics and ribbons
- felt, chiffon, silk, lace, wool and cellophane
- assortment of artificial berries, acorns or small fruits
- small Christmas decorations made from wood, tin or papier mâché
- silk or felt hearts (see page 70)
- glitter glue

1 Cut strips of rag in Christmas colours from tartans, metallic fabrics and bright and gaudy chiffons and silks. Hook the rag strips, along with ribbons, wool, lace or cellophane, through the cane wreath base and secure with simple knots. Continue until the wreath is covered.

2 Envelop the beads in fine fabric and secure the gathers around the top with embroidery silk or a thin piece of chiffon. Tie them singly or in clusters around the wreath or between the cane.

3 Tie artificial berries, acorns or fruits between the fabric beads, keeping an even distribution of texture around the wreath. If necessary, pierce the plastic decorations and thread through embroidery silk.

4 Cover the bangle or bracelet in tiny scraps of knotted rag, wool and silk. Using decorative ribbon or rag, tie the bracelet to the top of the ring in the centre so it hangs well.

5 Tie the Christmas decorations round the wreath. Attach the felt or silk hearts, and dab glitter glue in jewel-like droplets to brighten any dull areas.

TIP
Use the technique for making the padded hearts on page 70 to make padded Christmas trees, stars or other shapes.

The festive appearance of this wreath is achieved through the use of predominantly red and green fabrics, with Christmas ornaments and winter berries adding embellishment.

Decorative Household Objects

Transforming ordinary objects into sumptuous rag-decorated works of art is easy: your only limitation is the range of fabric you have collected. A silky tartan plate or an Indian paisley bowl can add handsome tone and texture to your interior colour scheme. Indulge in the fun of creating sunny little spotted pots and jugs, or exotically coloured matching eggs and egg cups to brighten a kitchen window-sill.

CHOOSING OBJECTS TO DECORATE

China, enamel, wood, plastic or pottery objects can all be covered with fabric. Collect old or used egg cups, trays, mugs, jugs, vases, bowls and plates to use for your rag decoration. Scour junk shops and jumble sales for chipped and stained enamel plates, dishes and bowls. New enamel pieces can be bought for a modest sum from hardware suppliers. Exquisitely shaped Art Deco bowls and vases can be found inexpensively if they have fine cracks, crazing, stains or an uninteresting plain surface. Wooden or plastic napkin rings, plastic egg cups and tin or wooden trays all have the potential to be transformed by rag craft into highly decorative items.

USING FABRIC

Choose your fabrics to blend in with the style and colours of the room in which they will be displayed, or make special pieces to give as presents. Use light-weight fabrics for covering objects such as plates, jugs, bowls or eggs because it is easier to manipulate and overlap than bulkier fabrics. Use heavier fabrics for more textured work, such as the papier mâché bowl on pages 88–9. Also cut out motifs such as flowers and leaves from large-patterned fabrics; these can be stuck down on trays or bowls to create a découpage effect or a carefully designed pattern.

Rag-decorated egg cups that match or contrast with the fabric of a covered egg make an interesting textural combination for display in your home or as a special gift. China napkin rings bound with delicate, richly coloured floral fabrics are an intriguing addition to a table setting, and can be designed to blend with a favourite tablecloth or to match a dinner service or tea plates.

VARNISHING FABRIC-COVERED OBJECTS

All the projects on the following pages and many throughout the book are sealed with an application of spray varnish or cold glaze to protect the decoration from marks and stains.

Spray varnishes are available in matt, gloss and satin finishes and deciding which one to use is a matter of personal choice.

Cold glaze, a water-based sealant, is available from pottery suppliers and some craft shops in matt, semi-shiny and gloss finishes. It is more hardwearing than spray varnish and the milky-looking sealant dries to a hard, clear finish. The glaze should be applied with a large, soft brush. To clean the brushes, simply rinse in warm water.

An array of old household items transformed with a covering of fabric. The bowl is papier mâché, decorated with pieces of fabric, and rag beads.

MOSAIC-EFFECT TRAY

This tray is decorated with random rag abstract shapes, a method adopted partly because of the interesting pattern they create but also because it would be difficult to stick one large piece of fabric to the surface without creating air bubbles. The wooden tray was very badly stained, and the rag strips usefully cover up the marks, as well as accentuate the lovely shape and gentle slope of the handles. You may like to use a tin tray; although tin trays lack the splendid dimensions and feel of wood, they are inexpensive and available in a variety of shapes.

The fabrics used here were plain-coloured cotton scraps taken from a sample book, which were then hand-printed with a natural sponge using acrylic paints (see pages 114–5). However, you could use any fabrics you like.

DECORATING THE TRAY

The mottled colouring of the fabric used in this project creates a rustic tile effect; marbled fabric (see pages 116–9) would be another excellent choice.

MATERIALS
- wooden or metal tray
- metal primer if using a metal tray
- gold (or other colour) acrylic paint for background
- dry glue stick
- printed fabric pieces
- spray varnish or cold glaze

1 Clean and lightly sand the wooden tray to rub back any glossy finish and produce a smooth surface on which to paint. For a metal tray, clean well, apply a coat of metal primer and allow to dry thoroughly. When the tray is prepared for painting, apply one coat of gold paint, then leave to dry.

2 Cut a number of oblong pieces of fabric of varying sizes. Arrange them on the tray to create an interlinking pattern. Leave a little space between each piece so the gold is revealed. Cut more oblong shapes as you progress, making sure the overall design is varied in shape and colour.

Cut narrow strips of rag for the edge of the tray. Cut small circles of rag using a hole punch to intersperse between the strips along the edge.

3 Stick down one fabric piece at a time with the dry glue stick, pressing out any air bubbles. Continue until the surface and edges of the tray are covered.

4 Seal the tray with an application of spray varnish or brush on a coat of cold glaze. If the tray will receive heavy use, apply two or three more coats of cold glaze or spray varnish to ensure the surface decoration is completely protected.

Worked in a limited range of colours and reminiscent of Italian tiles, this tray shows how a strong, graphic design can be achieved by carefully composing fabric pieces.

FABRIC EGGS

The dazzling, finished effect of a bowl sumptuously piled high with fabric-decorated eggs can be more beautiful than you could imagine. Use the richest crêpe ladies' handkerchiefs you can find; the ones used here were produced in the 1930s and 1940s in a striking range of beautifully coloured patterns. When choosing fabrics, look for the smallest patterns possible, try to avoid any with too much white background, and don't worry about the odd stain, hole or any other sign of wear and tear. Just select a fine, richly patterned palette of fabrics.

Most of the eggs illustrated here are made of polystyrene, and are available from a good craft supplier. They are ideal because they are durable, firm and easy to use. The remaining few are real blown eggs, and the advantage of these is their low cost, easy availability and they also give you the pleasure of conserving raw materials.

Artificial eggs are also produced in compressed cotton, again available from craft suppliers, but this material tends to have a slightly uneven surface.

HAND-BLOWN EGGS

To hand-blow an egg, begin by making a large hole with a hat pin or darning needle at the top and bottom of an egg. Holding the egg over a small bowl, blow hard through the top hole to remove the yoke, taking care not to crush the egg with your hands. You may find it helpful to make the bottom hole slightly larger than the top hole. Rinse the egg by holding the top hole gently under running water, then blow the water through; continue rinsing the egg until the water runs out clear.

MATERIALS
- Polystyrene or hand-blown eggs
- Dry glue stick
- Crêpe silk patterned fabric
- Sharp scissors
- Cold glaze or spray varnish

1 Cut a circle of fabric just a little larger than needed to encompass the whole egg.

2 Completely cover the egg smoothly and evenly with glue from a dry glue stick.

3 Place the egg on the centre of the wrong side of the fabric, then pull the fabric up tightly around the egg and gather it at the top.

4 The fabric will bunch up into folds which need to be removed. Snip these off one at a time, laying the fabric flat against the egg and making sure that the cut edges just touch, ideally with no overlap. To ensure an accurate join, cut the folds one at a time in succession. Smooth down the edges, making sure that they meet.

5 When the wrapped egg is perfectly smooth and the glue is dry, seal with a coat of cold glaze or spray varnish.

Display silk-covered eggs in a bowl, on a rack or hanging from banisters in a prominent place for all who see them to enjoy. They make an especially attractive centrepiece for Easter.

DISPLAYING THE EGGS

There are many ways of displaying the finished eggs; the simplest is to keep a collection in a bowl, a basket or a glass jar. Try covering an enamel or china dish in a toning fabric (see page 86), or create your own bowl with beautiful materials (see pages 88–9).

Eggs can be threaded with embroidery silk or very thin decorative cord and hung in clusters. For polystyrene eggs, thread a needle with embroidery silk, and push this right through the top section of the egg and out the other side; then pull both ends of the thread to the top, and the egg is ready to hang.

A blown egg is a little more difficult, and will need a piece of thread tied around the centre of a matchstick. Push this gently through the hole at the top of the egg, turning the match as it drops so it lodges across the width of the egg.

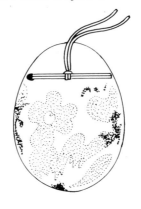

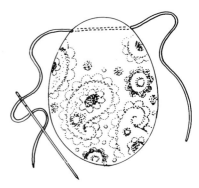

Below: To hang a polystyrene egg, thread a needle with embroidery silk and push it through the top of the egg.

Above: For a hand-blown egg, tie thread around the centre of a matchstick. Push the matchstick gently through the hole at the top and turn it so it lodges across the width of the egg.

FABRIC-COVERED PLATES AND JUGS

Old plates and jugs can be transformed by covering them with fabric. The 1940s produced a plethora of stencilled napkins and tablecloths, or you could choose tartans, florals or abstract designs.

COVERING AN ENAMEL PLATE
Avoid heavy weights of fabric, and consider the fabric design and where it would best be positioned on the plate.

MATERIALS
- enamel plate
- dry glue stick
- fabric slightly larger than the plate
- enamel paint in colour to tone with the fabric
- cold glaze or spray varnish

1 Clean and dry the plate to provide a good surface for gluing the fabric. Place the plate face down on the wrong side of the fabric, and draw round the edge with a pencil. Cut 5cm (2in) outside this line.

2 Glue the entire surface of the plate smoothly and evenly with the glue stick, including the rim and just underneath the edge. Check that no area is left unglued, because this will cause air bubbles.

3 Lay the fabric across the entire plate, gently easing and pressing it into place, working from the centre out. There should be no folds or creases at all. Tuck the fabric over the edge of the plate and press the edges down firmly; there will be some overlapping of fabric.

4 Turn the plate over and, using enamel paints, paint the base up to the join of the fabric. Leave to dry. Finish with spray varnish or cold glaze.

COVERING A JUG
Jugs decorated with rich, earthy fruit or flower fabrics can be used to display fruit, artificial berries or silk flowers. Choose any colours and designs of fabric you like, but you need to use a lightweight fabric.

MATERIALS
- enamel or china jug
- dry glue stick
- fabric slightly larger than the jug
- cold glaze or spray varnish

1 Clean and dry the jug to provide a good surface for gluing on fabric. Cut the fabric a little larger than the object to be decorated.

2 First cover the handle. Cut a strip of fabric wide enough to wrap round the thickness of the handle. Apply dry glue stick to the handle. Place the fabric lengthways on the handle so the joins meet inside, facing the jug. If necessary, snip the fabric where the handle joins the jug so the fabric smooths down.

3 Then cover the entire surface of the jug with a layer of glue stick. If the jug is very large or intricate, the glue could dry out before you have finished, so just work on one section at a time.

4 Place the object on the centre of the wrong side of the fabric. Stretch the fabric up around the jug. For difficult areas such as around handles or the deep curve of a bowl, cut a narrow V-shape out of the fabric and position the cut edges together so they just meet. Very fine, highly patterned fabrics will absorb the effect of small overlaps.

5 At the top of the jug, smooth the fabric over the rim to the inside of the jug, pressing down along the edge to secure the fabric. Seal with an application of spray varnish or a coat of cold glaze.

Covering plates and jugs with fabric creates a textural effect that is unmatched by painting techniques. Although not waterproof, the objects are ideal for artificial arrangements.

PAPIER MACHE AND RAG BOWL

Papier mâché is the perfect exercise in recycling, building up shapes and creating wild textures through the use of old newspapers and wallpaper paste. The final layer is an exciting blend of fabric, foil, beads and mirrored pieces. Because the papier mâché is soft, embroidery stitches can be sewn along the rim. The vast textural and decorative range of these materials is so much greater than simple paint and paper.

DESIGN INSPIRATION

Visit textile and embroidery exhibitions to see how artists blend texture, colour and stitching. Or investigate ethnic and folk art for creative ideas.

Indian Banjara embroidery is especially inspiring. It is a predominantly red fabric that is embroidered with bright colours in bold geometric blocks and zigzags. Its rich texture is augmented by tassels, mirrors and pieces of metal, which make it perfect for translating into a mixed-media papier mâché bowl.

PLANNING THE DECORATION

Consider how you will apply your fabric and achieve texture. Fabric pieces can be applied as part of an ordered composition, pieced together like a patchwork, or long strips laid next to each other.

Look at the fabric you are using for shapes or patterns that you could enhance with embroidery stitches, beads, buttons, sequins or foil. The rim of the bowl could be accentuated by soft woollen blanket stitch, silk chain stitch or feather stitch. If you prefer not to embroider onto the bowl, use scraps of embroidered fabrics to create texture.

APPLYING THE DECORATION

Use a latex adhesive to apply most fabrics to the bowl; however, use dry glue stick for fine silks, chiffons and lace so that no adhesive can seep through and mar the fabric. Heavy beads, foil, metal or mirror pieces may need a PVA white glue or an epoxy resin to ensure they stay firmly adhered. Small beads, sequins or buttons can be glued or sewn on.

MAKING A COLLECTION OF BOWLS

To produce a number of small papier mâché bowls, use disposable waxed paper dishes as a foundation for papier mâché. Working all the bowls at the same time, apply the first layer as described in steps 3 and 4 for the large bowl, but use PVA glue to make sure the strips adhere to the waxed surface. Leave to dry, then apply three more two-step layers, leaving until dry. Decorate all the bowls at once using the same fabrics.

MAKING THE DECORATED BOWL

Although papier mâché dries slowly this will leave you ample opportunity to plan the final decoration.

MATERIALS
- large mixing bowl or dish for a mould
- petroleum jelly or plastic wrap
- newspaper
- non-toxic cellulose wallpaper paste
- white spirit and cotton wool or a soft rag
- scissors
- acrylic or emulsion paint
- fabric scraps, lace, net and ribbon
- beads, buttons, sequins, foil and metal pieces
- woollen yarn or embroidery silk and needle
- latex glue or dry glue stick
- PVA glue or epoxy resin adhesive
- spray varnish or cold glaze

1 Coat the inside and rim of the bowl with petroleum jelly or tightly wrap the bowl in plastic wrap; this prevents the pasted strips sticking to the mould and helps release the papier mâché shape.

2 Cut newspaper into 5cm (2in) wide strips. Mix the wallpaper paste according to the manufacturer's instructions.

3 Coat the newspaper strips in a little paste and place them on the bowl in rows, overlapping the rim and covering the inner surface of the bowl.

4 Apply a second layer of pasted strips at right angles to the previous layer; this will give stability and strength to the bowl. Repeat this two-layer process eight times. Leave in a warm place until completely dry; this may take several days.

5 Gently remove the shape from the mould, helping it out with a palette knife, if necessary. Remove any traces of petroleum jelly with white spirit.

6 Neatly trim the rim of the bowl with a pair of scissors. To tidy the cut edge, apply very small pasted strips over the rim and leave again until dry.

7 Apply a coat of paint over the bowl; this will prevent the adhesive used for attaching the decoration from being absorbed into the surface. Leave to dry.

8 Now glue the fabric to the bowl. The fabrics could be applied as part of a design, in a patchwork of scraps, or as long strips laid alongside each other. Stick down any heavy beads and metal or mirror pieces using PVA white glue or epoxy resin adhesive. Leave to dry.

9 Seal the bowl with an application of spray varnish or a coat of cold glaze. After the varnish has dried, decorate the rim with a blanket stitch by piercing through the papier mâché with the needle.

Papier mâché lends itself to the most extravagant of decoration. These bowls show how fabric, beads, foil and embroidery can be integrated into spectacular works of art.

Beads, Buttons and Jewellery

Making your own beads, buttons and jewellery with fabric scraps will enable you to devise the most exciting and unusual ornaments. Decorated buttons and beads can be used to add rich detail and texture to all types of rag projects, or to customize existing items such as bags, hats, clothes and soft furnishings. Hand-decorated buttons can imbue a woollen cardigan or jacket with an unique personal quality. Bracelets, necklaces, earrings and brooches can be made from special pieces of fabric or decorated beads and buttons.

CHOOSING MATERIALS

Dive into your rag basket and pick out the most vibrant and intense colours, the tiniest of intricate patterns, or a blend of muted and delicate shades if your taste inclines towards softer tones. When choosing fabric for jewellery projects, you may like to select those which complement your clothes.

Beads can be made from such diverse materials as pieces of balsa wood, polystyrene balls, plastic tubing and fabric itself. Save all the old buttons from the clothing and rags and keep the useful and pretty ones. Thick, plain buttons can be a good base for painting a simple folk decoration, embossed buttons can be subtly highlighted with paint and old fabric buttons can easily be re-covered with richly coloured or embroidered scraps.

Jewellery findings will be needed for many of the projects in this chapter. They are available from specialist bead shops and some craft suppliers, and there are suitable findings for every purpose – whether you need necklace and bracelet clasps, spacers, or pierced or clip earrings and studs or hooks. Thin wire can be substituted for some of the findings, but it is really worth searching for the professional versions as they are not expensive.

Only the smallest pieces of rag are needed to create unique beads, buttons and jewellery. Tiny prints and intense colours provide much impact, and produce sensational pieces.

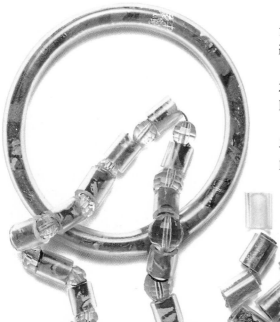

BEADS

Rag-decorated beads have a soft, textured interest that surpasses the designs of many ordinary manufactured beads. Beads are always useful to have at hand for craft projects, and the following techniques will help you create a varied collection.

CLEAR PLASTIC BEADS

These beads are made by filling a length of clear plastic tubing, such as the kind used for wine-making, with vivid little rag pieces. This technique produces an intriguing bead with hidden and textured depths.

The ideal fabrics to use are net, chiffon, satin and glittery metallic materials, and choose the most exciting colour combinations you can find. The more contrast in the textures of the scraps, the more fascinating the beads will look. You will need to use a needle and thread to string the beads, sewing through the fabric in each tube.

MATERIALS
- clear plastic tubing
- variety of exotic fabric scraps
- clear glue

1 Cut the tubing into small strips to represent each individual bead.

2 Select small colourful scraps, and roll up each little piece.

3 Squeeze a small dab of glue into each tube, then push in the pieces of rolled-up fabric.

BALSA WOOD BEADS

Balsa wood is extremely easy to cut and pierce, making it an excellent material for bead-making. Because the wood is so light, these beads would be ideal for dangly earrings.

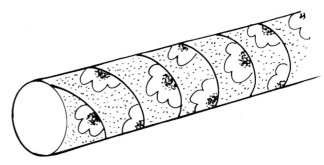

MATERIALS
- colourful patterned fabric
- length of balsa wood dowelling, about 8mm ($\frac{1}{4}$in) in diameter
- latex adhesive or dry glue stick
- craft knife or scalpel
- acrylic paint
- jewellery screwdriver, bodkin or tapestry needle
- length of wire, strong nylon thread or fishing line
- cold glaze

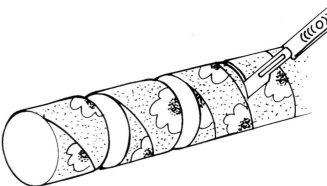

1 Cut the fabric into a long strip and wind it into a ball. Cover the dowelling with glue; use glue stick if the fabric is fine and delicate, but latex adhesive if the fabric is a thicker cotton.

2 Lightly press the end of the rag strip to one end of the dowelling. Wind the fabric round the stick, bandage fashion, until the dowelling is completely bound with rag. If latex adhesive has been used, leave to dry.

Balsa wood and fabric-covered beads make chunky but lightweight beads, which are ideal for making into jewellery.

3 With the craft knife or scalpel blade, gently slice through the fabric-covered dowel at equal intervals to create the beads. Paint the ends of each bead with acrylics in a toning colour.

4 When the paint is dry, make a hole through each bead using a fine jeweller's screwdriver, a bodkin or a tapestry needle. Thread the beads onto a length of wire, leaving a large space between each bead. Hang from a coat-hanger, hook or drawing pin.

5 Seal the beads with cold glaze to protect them from dirt and dust and prevent loose edges from unravelling. When dry, slip the beads off the wire.

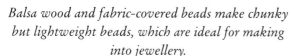

FABRIC-COVERED BEADS

Polystyrene and compressed cotton balls are perfect for covering with small, beautifully detailed pieces of fabric, and are available from most craft suppliers.

Wooden beads can also be used; damaged beaded car-seat covers are a good source. If you do wrap fabric around beads that have holes, make a snip through the fabric at each hole so you can thread the beads.

MATERIALS
- polystyrene or wooden beads
- dry glue stick
- fine cotton or flowered crêpe, or a fine piece of sponged or marbled fabric
- large needle or bodkin
- length of wire
- cold glaze or spray varnish

1 Cut pieces of fabric, each large enough to comfortably wrap round a polystyrene ball.

2 Cover the balls with a thick coat of glue stick. Slowly envelop each ball in rag, as described for Fabric Eggs on page 84.

3 Pierce the polystyrene balls with a bodkin or large needle and thread onto wire, leaving a space between each ball.

4 Hang the wire from a coat-hanger or hook, and seal with a coat of cold glaze or spray varnish. Leave to dry, then slip the beads off the wire.

ROLLED FABRIC BEADS

Pretty oval beads can be produced from long, narrow, triangular-shaped pieces of fabric. This method is traditionally used for paper beads: the fabric is wound round a cocktail stick, but you could also use wire.

MATERIALS
- firm cotton pieces
- cocktail sticks
- dry glue stick
- cold glaze or spray varnish

1 Cut the fabric in an elongated triangle (see below), approximately 3cm (1¼in) wide and 18cm (7in) long, narrowing off to a point.

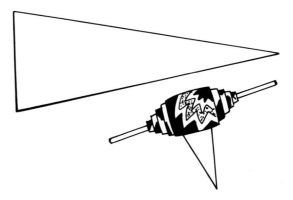

2 Lay the triangular strip on a flat surface, dab a little glue on the wide end and place the cocktail stick along the edge.

3 Roll the fabric from the wide end, winding tightly and evenly. Glue the triangular tip to the roll to hold the bead together.

4 Embed one end of the cocktail stick in modelling clay or a compressed paper egg carton. Seal the bead with cold glaze or spray varnish, and leave to dry.

5 Carefully slide the fabric bead from the stick.

Rolled fabric beads look particularly attractive when made into long necklaces with smaller, round beads as spacers.

BUTTONS

Old buttons are often available in jars from jumble sales, and they can be given a personal touch by adding paintwork or by covering them with fabric. You might like to customize beads for using on a special item of clothing, or simply decorate a quantity to have for sewing projects.

PAINTED BUTTONS

Plain buttons can be transformed by imaginative paint effects. This dazzling selection shows the vast range of design ideas possible.

Decorative effects can be easily added to buttons using enamel, oil or acrylic paints. Look in local museums, antique shops or libraries for examples of East European folk art, primitive art and crafts, and barge and canal painting. All these have an unassuming charm and gaiety of colour that can be usefully imitated when painting your own buttons.

HIGHLIGHTING EFFECTS

Embossed buttons will generally look livelier if the raised areas are subtly highlighted, revealing a design. Use a thin wash of acrylic or metallic paint, gently dragged across the surface of the button.

Add more detailed highlighting by rubbing over relief areas with gilt wax, applied with your finger.

FLORAL AND ABSTRACT DESIGNS

Naive representations of flowers have a charm of their own and need a minimum of artistic skill. Simple abstract designs, such as little zig-zags, stripes or colourful dots, have a striking, graphic quality.

SPONGING EFFECTS

Sponged buttons are a wonderfully simple way of adding a designer touch to blend perfectly with the yarn colours of hand-knitting.

MATERIALS
- solid plain buttons
- acrylic or artists' oil paints
- paint brush and natural sponge
- cold glaze and a soft brush

1 Paint the first colour onto the sponge with a brush. Dab any excess paint onto scrap paper. Using gentle pressure, dab the sponge onto the button. Leave to dry.

2 Repeat step 1 with the second colour.

3 Seal with cold glaze, using a very soft brush to avoid brush strokes.

FABRIC-COVERED BUTTONS

Use old fabric-covered buttons or buy new, ready-to-cover blanks for this project. The blanks are easy to cover, and usually have a serrated edge to grip the fabric. You could also cover plastic or metal buttons.

This is a good opportunity to use up minuscule scraps of small checks, tartan and tiny flowers. Fabrics which have been embroidered with a tiny motif make a particularly exquisite covering.

Use intricate motifs, small-scale patterns and the best part of embroidered fabric scraps to cover old buttons or button blanks.

MATERIALS
- old buttons with shanks
- lightweight, delicate fabric
- sewing thread and needle

1 Cut a circle of delicate fabric a little larger than the button. Sew a running stitch round the edge.

2 Pull the stitches to gather, insert the button inside the centre, then pull the stitches tightly until the front of the button looks taut and neat.

3 Knot the thread tightly. If necessary, stitch the gathered fabric together on the back of the button to secure more firmly.

NECKLACES

Any of the beads on pages 91-3 can be strung into a necklace. Look for old necklaces that can be broken up – the beads can be used as spacers between the rag-decorated beads. Save any old fasteners and clasps for re-use – although bead shops and most good craft shops stock a range of beads and jewellery findings.

Thread for stringing beads is available in nylon, silk and cotton, and also in the simplest of leather thonging. Thonging is available in a variety of colours, and is perfect for an ethnic look if the holes in your beads are large enough. It does not need a clasp and can simply be tied around the neck.

DESIGNING A NECKLACE

Consider the design of your necklace in terms of the whole shape. Do you want even-sized beads, or do you want larger dazzling beads in the centre graduating to smaller ones at the end? To do justice to the beauty of rag-decorated beads, you may need to separate them with plain beads or metallic bead caps. Use a special bead tray or arrange the beads in a straight line on non-slip fabric to plan the design.

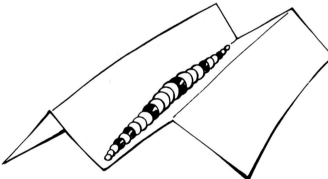

Small beads look stunning when strung on fine silk thread, but you could also make a pendant by looping a few large beads through a leather thong.

MAKING A NECKLACE

Make a bead tray by creasing a piece of paper or card in concertina folds; alternatively, use a piece of corrugated cardboard.

MATERIALS
- rag-decorated beads and spacers
- nylon, silk or cotton stringing thread
- necklace clasp fitting
- clear glue

1 Arrange the beads in an attractive design, as described above.

2 Calculate the length of the necklace and cut the thread at least $2^{1}/_{2}$ times this size. Fold the thread in half, loop it twice through the clasp or ring and knot tightly.

3 Thread the beads onto the doubled thread; use a needle if the thread is cotton or silk.

4 When all the beads are strung, loop the thread twice through the other half of the clasp and knot. Take the thread back through a few of the beads, tying it in another knot to secure firmly.

5 Trim and seal the knots with the clear glue.

TIP

Hand-crafted rag beads can also be strung onto hat elastic or several strands of shirring elastic to create bracelets that will fit any size of wrist.

A great variety of necklace designs can be created with rag beads. Soft, pastel, floral beads or textured ethnic beads are all stylish in different ways.

EARRINGS

The following projects use beads, buttons and rag strips to make earrings. Further embellishments can be made to the fabric, such as stripes or zigzags in acrylic paint or embroidery with lurex or thick silk thread. You may like to choose materials and decorations that tone with your favourite clothes.

For dangly earrings, link straight wires and jump rings in series to give the earrings an attractive 'swing' when worn.

For the button earrings, choose earrings with flat backs so they adhere successfully to clip fittings. Particularly effective are colourful 1940s and '50s cut-out plastic buttons, embossed metallic or wooden buttons, or patterned enamel buttons.

DROP EARRINGS

You could use several fabric beads in gradating sizes for each of these earrings.

MATERIALS
- wire or headpins
- fabric beads and small coloured beads
- small round-nose pliers
- jump rings and earring hooks

1 Thread a fabric bead onto each headpin or a length of wire that has been looped at the bottom.

2 Trim the headpins or wires and bend back with pliers to make a loop at the top of each bead. Link another looped wire into each top loop.

3 Thread a few smaller beads onto each new wire. Trim and bend back with pliers to make a loop at the top of each earring. Link a jump ring through each loop, then link an earring hook through each jump ring.

HOOP EARRINGS

If these earrings are too flashy and highly decorated for your tastes, bind the hoops with plain-coloured ribbon or fabric strips.

MATERIALS
- plastic curtain rings or cut-out cardboard hoops
- interesting fabric strips or ribbon
- dry glue stick
- beads, sequins, embroidery thread or glitter glue, to decorate
- jump rings and earring hooks
- small round-nose pliers
- cold glaze or spray varnish

1 Using dry glue stick to secure the fabric, wrap narrow strips of rag round the plastic curtain rings or cardboard hoops.

2 Decorate with paint, thick drops of glitter glue, embroidery or glued or sewn-on sequins and tiny beads. Seal with cold glaze or spray varnish and leave to dry.

3 Attach a large jump ring around each hoop, using a small pair of pliers if necessary. Insert earring hooks through the jump rings.

BUTTON EARRINGS

Painted or fabric covered buttons make charming clip-on earrings, but you can also glue tiny painted buttons onto pierced stud earring findings.

MATERIALS
- pairs of matching buttons with flat backs
- clip-on earring fittings
- superglue, or two-part epoxy resin adhesive

1 Decorate the buttons as described on pages 94–5.

2 Glue the buttons to the clip-on fittings with superglue or two-part epoxy resin, following the manufacturer's instructions. Leave to dry.

A superb selection of fashionable earrings is shown here, from drop beaded earings and rag-bound hoop earrings to clip-on button earrings.

TIP

Small, neat brooches can be made in much the same way as the earrings. Attach a safety pin or brooch pin to the back of the button by sewing through the button holes. Secure the thread with a dab of glue.

99

BRACELETS

Rag-decorated bracelets and bangles can be quick and pleasurable to make, and provide a wonderful opportunity to show off those special little scraps you have tucked away. Plain plastic bangles covered in rich fabric look fascinatingly exotic and different. Motifs can be cut from fabric and glued onto wide coloured bangles, and tubing can be filled with colourful rag to make a bracelet.

BASIC MATERIALS

Plain plastic bangles are often available from charity shops and jumble sales. If finding a large quantity of plain bangles is difficult, cut up a washing-up liquid bottle in circular strips to the width you require. These strips can be covered with thick fabrics or strips of embroidery, but if the fabrics are fine, you may need to build up on the plastic band with layers of paste and newspaper to form a papier mâché bangle (see pages 88–9).

Fabrics can be as wild as you like! Strips of tie-dyed or marbled fabric, pieces of ribbon and decorated braid, vibrant and patterned cottons, silk ties and scarves, strips of embroidery and chiffon scarves with metallic thread can be used to great effect.

DECORATING TECHNIQUES

Wrapped bangles can be made by winding rag strips, bandage fashion, round a bangle, gluing the beginning and end with glue stick so it does not unravel. Further decoration can be added with an exciting touch to the centre, such as a jewel stitched onto a piece of dyed lace or a row of colourful buttons.

Striped bangles can be made by using a variety of individually patterned and coloured strips. Cut the strips to double the width of the bangle, wrap round the bangle and glue in place.

Small-scale fabric motifs can be cut from a decorative fabric and glued on a broad metallic or plainly-coloured plastic bangle in an attractive design.

TEXTILE BRACELET

Any embroidered textile is suitable for this project, from bold, ethnic designs to delicate all-over florals.

MATERIALS
- wide plain plastic bangle
- thick piece of embroidery, smocking or appliqué textile
- dry glue stick
- cold glaze or spray varnish

1 Cut the fabric into a long strip that is about the same width as that of the bangle. Completely cover the wrong side of the fabric with a light application of dry glue stick.

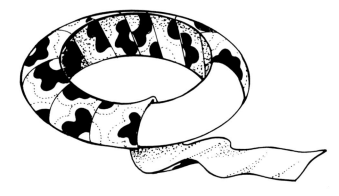

2 Press one end of the strip to the inside of the bangle and begin to wind the fabric around the bracelet. When the bangle is covered, pull the strip to the bracelet back, trim off and secure the end.

3 Seal with cold glaze or spray varnish.

SEE-THROUGH TUBE BRACELET

As this bracelet could never be mistaken for being chic, indulge in shocking pinks, lime greens, neon oranges or other jazzy and fun colours of fabric.

MATERIALS
- plastic tubing
- very small, bright pieces of silk, chiffon, ribbon, metallic scraps, net or assorted wrappings
- knitting needle
- small piece of balsa wood or cork
- acrylic or emulsion paint
- PVA adhesive
- masking tape

1 Cut a length of plastic tubing to fit comfortably around the wrist.

2 Push very small pieces of scrunched-up fabric through the tube with a knitting needle. Set aside.

3 Cut the balsa wood or cork to fit firmly into both ends of the tubing. Paint with acrylics or emulsion and leave to dry.

4 Dab the painted plug with PVA adhesive and join the tube ends with the plug. Hold the join with masking tape until the glue is dry.

TIP
A rolled strip of coloured compressed paper can also be used as a plug.

Re-using Knitwear

Old and worn knitted sweaters, scarves, gloves and socks, or unfinished knitting projects, can be made into cushions, blankets, framed pictures or used to customize existing items. Choose rich stripes, folky designs or the strongest patterns you can find. Also look for pieces of solidly coloured knitwear that can be patched together in exciting colour combinations or used to break up and offset strong patterns.

USING AND CHOOSING KNITWEAR PIECES

Re-using knitwear is an area of recycling that is relatively unexplored, since the possibility of knitted pieces unravelling has been enough to deter most artists and craftspeople from developing ideas in this field. However, most of the pieces used in the projects on the following pages were prevented from fraying with latex adhesive, making endless blanket-stitching or zig-zag stitching unnecessary.

Like all specialized aspects of rag collecting, it is just a matter of tuning in to another texture. Begin by looking for the more obviously suitable articles such as richly coloured sweaters or slip covers with rows of small, beautifully worked patterns. Sumptuous Fair Isle and Peruvian sweaters have enormous potential. Some of the wilder colours and designs are found in children's garments, so look out for out-grown or shrunken sweaters, so many of which are abandoned at local jumble sales (see pages 10-11 for more information on sourcing knitwear).

CUSTOMIZING CLOTHES

Clothes can be delightfully customized with the addition of knitted patches. You could even create an entire waistcoat, shawl or winter scarf from a patchwork of pieces. An old denim or tweed jacket can be given a designer's touch by covering the collar and cuffs with a fine piece of Fair Isle or vividly coloured Peruvian knitting.

Choose the woollen scraps according to the weight of the clothes you are customizing; heavy fabrics such as denim can take bulkier knits, whereas clothes made from lightweight fabrics need more delicate pieces. Consider the colours of your knitted pieces too, choosing those that enhance the clothes.

DECORATING BABY CLOTHES

Babies' jackets look especially charming when customized with a delicate, soft piece of knitting in a pastel shade. Two squares of knitting, such as those taken from an faded, soft sweater, can be sewn together to make a baby's bonnet, with a pretty plaited yarn attached for the tie and a bobble at the top.

HANDBAGS AND HATS

Knitted motifs or scraps can be sewn onto cloth handbags, satchels and hats to add a special personal touch to factory-made items. A small square of knitting makes a beautiful little pocket when sewn on to a rucksack, and long strips of closely-woven knitwear that have exciting designs make a perfect border for the handle or top opening of a cloth bag.

Pieces cut from heavy blankets, lined with fabric and embellished with embroidery stitches, can be made into tote bags, cosmetics bags or tiny purses.

CUSHIONS AND COVERINGS

Child-size sweaters in bright colours are perfect for making into hot-water bottle covers or travel-size cushions for the car or airplane. For a cushion, just follow the instructions for the Woollen Cushion on pages 104-5, substituting a child's sweater for an adult-size one. For the hot-water bottle cover, the side seams and arms can be cut off and then the sweater stitched all round the straight edges, leaving the neck as the outlet for the top of the bottle.

This randomly pieced patchwork of knitted shapes incorporates a diversity of designs, and exhibits the breadth of knitwear that is available.

Woollen Cushions

The large areas of knitting at the front and back of an adult-size sweater can be made up into cushions, as shown in this project. The arms and any other offcuts you don't need can be saved for other projects. Before you begin, you will need to assess the size of the finished cushion by measuring the largest area you can cut from the front of the sweater. A cushion pad should be bought to fit a little smaller than this size to allow for seams.

Sweaters with interesting patterns or textures make incredibly stunning cushions. Simple stripes or checked sweaters also make delightful designs. The beauty of this project is that the real decoration is already there in the fabric you choose.

MATERIALS
- adult-size sweater
- latex adhesive
- pins
- darning wool and large needle
- cushion pad

1 Cut the largest area from the front and back of the sweater to make two equally sized squares, cutting off the side seams and arms, the collar and shoulders and any ribbing from the bottom.

2 Lay the two pieces side by side on a sheet of newspaper, and carefully and thoroughly coat all the raw edges with latex adhesive. Leave to dry.

Alternatively, stitch the raw edges by sewing firm running stitches around each piece. Then blanket-stitch the edges by hand or machine zig-zag. Take care while stitching that the piece of knitting is kept firm and is not stretched or pulled out of shape.

3 Now lay the two pieces together, right sides facing, and pin. Stitch three sides together and a little of the fourth, leaving a gap.

4 Turn right sides out, making sure the corners are pushed out; then slip in the cushion pad. Tuck the remaining raw edges to the inside and slip stitch to close the gap.

Use large pieces of knitwear or piece together small patches to make striking cushions like these here, that are sure to get attention.

WOOLLEN PATCHWORK

Creating patchwork blankets or cushions is a splendid way of making something useful and attractive from either plain or patterned woollen scraps. A blanket can be any size, and can be used as a throw-rug over chairs or sofas, or as a bed cover. A good idea is to begin with a small project such as a cushion to get a feel for working with knitted scraps. Two simple ideas can be developed: either make an even patchwork of linking squares or fashion your patchwork as a collection of randomly shaped scraps.

PIECED DESIGNS

A carefully pieced composition requires a little advance planning, and can be worked in much the same way as a patchwork quilt. Look at quilt designs, such as Log Cabin or stripey quilting, to see how the knitted pieces can be sewn together. Or use a simple design and achieve variety in the patterns of the knitted pieces you use, such as Fair Isle or stripes. Avoid using scraps that are too small, as you will find it tedious to sew them together. Rectangular strips or squares are the best shapes to use because there is less risk of the knitting pulling out of shape.

RANDOM DESIGNS

Random patchwork is an ideal way to use up the odd shapes of knitting sometimes left over after cutting a series of uniform squares from a garment. Cuffs, gloves, sleeves from toddler's sweaters and small knitted motifs can all join together in a glorious and extravagant array of colour. Any shapes can be used: just pin them together as you cut each piece, gradually building up an exciting piece of work that arises purely as a result of your own instinctive inclinations. The joins could be embroidered with a feather stitch so that the finished effect is reminiscent of Victorian silk patchwork.

USING A TEMPLATE FOR PATCHWORK

Use a ceramic tile or a strong card square to cut out woollen squares for patchworking. A tile is particularly useful because it presses the knitting so that it cannot be stretched while the square is being outlined.

PATCHWORK BLANKET

The juxtaposition of squares is important; some squares look exciting next to each other, while others look uninspiring.

MATERIALS
- ceramic tile or square card for template
- woollen rags
- water-soluble felt-tip pen
- pins
- darning wool and needle
- latex adhesive
- tapestry wool and needle
- narrow, ready-made woven binding
- pre-washed fabric for lining

1 Place the template on the knitting and draw round the square with a washable felt-tip pen. Cut out and repeat for as many squares as required.

2 Lay out all the squares and rearrange them until a pleasing balance of colour and design is achieved. A square blanket should have an equal number of squares across the width and length, and variations to the finished size of the blanket can be made by adjusting the number of squares.

3 Working one row at a time, pin, then hand-sew the pieces together using darning wool, making sure the squares are not stretched. When the squares in each row are stitched together, sew the rows together.

4 Turn the blanket over and press the seams.

The soft, muted colours in this patchwork blanket are in harmonious balance, and the combination of Fair Isle patterns with stripes adds interest.

5 Generously coat all the joins and the raw outside edges with latex adhesive. This may take several days to dry, so carry out the procedure where the blanket can be left undisturbed.

6 If desired, add an embroidered top stitch, for example, a simple chain or feather stitch, to define the patchwork joins. This can be worked using a tapestry wool that matches the colour of the binding. The stitches can be large and fairly crude, adding a charm that enhances the finished effect.

7 To finish the edges, pin the woven binding to the edges of the blanket, making sure all edges are parallel and exactly the same length. Hand-sew the binding in place.

8 Cut the backing fabric 1cm ($^1/_2$in) larger all round than the finished blanket. Turn under the seam allowance and press. Place right side up on the back of the blanket, pin the two pieces together and slip stitch the folded edges of the lining to the woven binding.

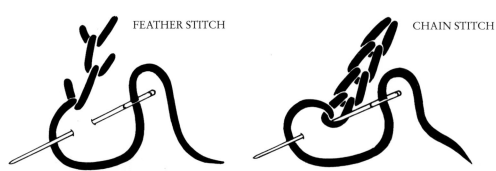

FEATHER STITCH

CHAIN STITCH

The woollen patches can be random in shape to give variety to the composition. You may like to add a topstitch between the squares for added emphasis.

FRAMED SAMPLES

Occasionally you come across a beautiful but worn hand-knitted sweater or waistcoat at a jumble sale that seems too stunning to cut into small pieces. By framing the piece, you can enjoy it on a daily basis.

The knitted scrap used in this project was a cardigan I never finished. However, I liked the muted colours and the folky little figures – and they seemed so appropriate for a country-style living-room. When I spotted the frame in a junk shop, the two seemed perfect for each other!

Look for old picture frames with or without glass. Glass usually deadens the impact of knitted texture, but bolder pieces of knitwear, maybe with rosy floral motifs, can be enhanced by a bright and glossily painted frame. The frames can be painted or left as they are. Choose a frame that is considerably smaller than your knitted piece.

MATERIALS
- frame
- strong card or cardboard
- piece of knitting
- dry glue stick
- fine pins
- hammer
- brown sticky paper tape

1 Cut the card to the size of the inner frame. Cover with glue stick and place the knitting on top. Trim, leaving enough fabric to take over the edges.

2 Apply glue around the edge of the back of the card. Cut slits in the corners of the excess fabric along the diagonal and stretch the fabric to the back, pressing it down to stick.

3 Secure the card in the frame with a few pins, then lightly tap it in along each edge with the hammer.

4 Place another piece of card or brown wrapping paper on the back of the frame, and tape down with brown sticky paper tape.

Show off a treasured textile by mounting it in a frame. Paint or gild the frame, if desired, but do not allow it to overpower the knit.

Dyeing, Printing and Marbling

Exciting effects are possible with dyeing, marbling and printing techniques, and your own hand-coloured fabrics add a new dimension to ragwork. Any new project you undertake can be specially designed from the fabric itself to the finished work, which not only makes the objects you create more special, but also allows you to cater individually for a finished result that is not possible using manufactured patterns and prints.

Tie-dyeing produces different tones and patterns, making perfect fabrics for hooked rag rugs or wall hangings. Printing is a more controlled method of adding decoration to fabric, and either large mottled effects or tiny repeat patterns can be created.

Marbling produces more spontaneous designs that can be as colourful or muted as you like.

Exceptionally beautiful designs can be framed, but all results are perfect for cutting into strips and using to add colourful tones and hues to ragwork.

DYEING FABRICS

Dyeing fabric for rag crafts means putting aside some of the traditional rules involved in dyeing techniques, especially the tedious stirring of dye-baths for hours on end! Instead of creating an even covering of colour, the aim is for the finished effect to be as patchy as possible. Fashioning items from strips of dyed rag creates a subtle and exciting random colour distribution, an effect which is specially desirable in rag rugs.

Once you are familiar with the effects of dyes, try mixing dye colours to create the intermediary shades you may need. Variations in tones will also be caused by the colour of the fabric you are dyeing. Try experimenting with, perhaps, a blue dye on pink and red fabrics to create delightful lavenders, plums and violets. Yellow dye on fabrics in shades of blue can produce a beautiful range of greens, from celery, sage, olive and apple to the richest of bottle and emerald green. Your colour experiments may create the most perfect complementary colours for you to work with, such as olive green with a deep red or terracotta.

DYEING TECHNIQUES

One-colour dyeing produces a range of tones of the same colour if the fabrics are added at different times, and this is the simplest method of dyeing. The aim is to use the dye until the palest shades are produced.

Tie-dyeing produces intriguing multicoloured effects. The fabric is folded, pleated or crumpled, and then knotted or bound tightly with string, elastic bands or raffia. The tied parts resist the dye, while the rest of the fabric absorbs the dye colour. Elaborate effects can be created by untying the fabric, re-tying in a different position, and dyeing in another colour; the colour overlap will create a third colour.

Bleach-dyeing is worked in a similar way to tie-dying, but a coloured fabric is tied and dipped into a bleaching agent to remove colour. You can use either hot or cold methods for one-colour and tie-dyeing.

BASIC MATERIALS

Synthetic fabric dyes can be found in hardware and craft shops in a wide variety of colours, and clear instructions are always included. A good idea is to buy a selection of basic primary colours and use them in combination to produce other colours. Although commercial dyes will give a recommendation for the amount of dye you need for a quantity of fabric, these quantities do not need to be followed for making fabrics to use in ragwork.

Use a huge old saucepan as a dye-bath; these can usually be found second-hand, and as the condition doesn't matter too much, the cost should be minimal.

CHOOSING FABRICS

Particularly good materials for dyeing include the following: fine lawn-cotton Indian dresses with pallid background colours; pieces of embroidered cotton tablecloths and babies' pillowslips; crocheted and lace synthetics; and mixtures such as polyester and cotton. If fabrics are new, they should be pre-washed and dried before use.

Begin your first dyeing efforts on white and cream backgrounds, to gauge the true depth and tone of your dye colours and to experiment with shades, much as you would try out paint.

ONE-COLOUR DYEING

Use this technique to dye fabrics in different shades of the same colour.

MATERIALS
- hot-water dye in any colour
- salt
- jug or bowl to mix dye in
- large pan for a dye-bath
- rubber or plastic gloves
- plastic or wooden spoon
- fabric scraps and trims

1 Wearing rubber gloves, mix the dye powder with boiling water and salt in a jug or bowl, following the manufacturer's instructions. Stir until the powder is completely dissolved.

2 Place the dye-bath container on the stove and pour in enough hot water to cover the fabrics. Add the dissolved dye, heating at a low temperature.

3 Wet the fabric. Put all the fabrics that require an intense depth of colour such as ribbons, lace and rags in the bath first; then, as the strength of the dye-bath weakens, add the remaining fabric.

4 Give the dye-bath an occasional stir with a wooden spoon and heat the water to simmering point, then take off the heat and leave the fabric in the dye for 15-20 minutes.

5 Press the fabrics tightly against the side of the dye-bath with the wooden spoon, then rinse thoroughly with lukewarm water. Wash the fabric gently in warm, soapy water and leave to dry.

BLEACH DYEING

The dye remover keeps the existing fabric colour in tied areas, while stripping colour from the rest.

MATERIALS
- pre-dye colour remover
- large pan for a dye-bath
- rubber or plastic gloves
- plastic or wooden spoon
- coloured cotton fabric

1 Prepare a solution of warm water and colour remover following the manufacturer's instructions.

2 Wet the coloured fabric. Tie or knot the fabric, as for tie-dyeing (see above).

3 Add the fabric to the dye-bath. Bring to the boil, stirring constantly. Take off the heat and leave immersed for 5–30 minutes, depending upon the amount and depth of colour to be removed.

4 Rinse well, then wash in hot, soapy water and rinse again thoroughly before allowing to dry. The dye will be resisted in the knotted areas.

TIE-DYEING

While most people are familiar with the basic tie-dye process, there are a surprising number of ways to create different patterns, such as tying pebbles into the cloth or using knotted rope.

MATERIALS
- cold-water dye in any colour
- dye fix or 1 tablespoon of washing soda
- cotton fabric
- salt
- string, elastic bands or raffia
- stones, marbles or corks
- rubber gloves

1 Mix the cold-water dye according to the manufacturer's instructions, adding the dye-fix or washing soda and salt as directed.

The way you tie or knot your fabric will determine the dyed pattern. Fabric can be neatly pleated, gently folded, knotted or simply crumpled.

2 Tie the fabric with string or elastic bands, pleating, knotting, bunching or wrapping it with stones, corks or pebbles.

3 Wet and wring out the tied fabric and immerse it in the prepared dye-bath. Stir occasionally. Leave until the fabrics are dyed to a slightly darker colour than desired, or follow the dye manufacturer's instructions.

4 Remove the fabric from the dye solution. Wash and rinse thoroughly before untying the knots. Wash the fabric with warm, soapy water, rinse again and leave to dry.

TIP
Use a hot-water dye for this method if you prefer, following the steps for One-Colour Dyeing. You can also use two or more dye-baths of colour to achieve more multicoloured effects.

Tie-dyed and bleach-dyed fabrics produce somewhat similar results. Particularly striking pieces can be used to cover objects, but even failures can be cut into strips and used in rag rugs.

PRINTING FABRICS

Printing can be a quick and effective way of breaking up a plain fabric, and small prints look beautiful in many rag craft projects. A printing stamp or block, or even a cork or other household item, is dipped into paint then stamped on the surface of the fabric.

Use closely woven fabrics such as cotton, silk and man-made materials for printing; rough fabrics will not take the detail of the impressions so well. Pre-wash new fabric and iron all your fabric. Although the decorated fabric for this project will not be washable, you could substitute fabric paints which allow the finished fabric to be washed.

INKS AND PAINTS

Water-based acrylic paints were used for the hand-block project below, but there are many other options. Special water-based textile printing inks and paints are the best choice, but follow the manufacturer's instructions carefully to ensure the colours stay fast. Artists' oil paints, diluted with a small amount of white spirit or turpentine, can also be used.

USING HOUSEHOLD OBJECTS AS STAMPS

Pencil ends, bottle tops, sticks, cotton reels, screws, nail heads, corks and a variety of lids and stoppers are just a few of the materials you can use for printing.

Erasures can be bought in a wide range of ready-cut shapes, such as Christmas trees, flowers, stars and so on, and are perfect to use as a printing stamp. Thinner, larger erasers can be cut into any shape with a craft knife, but obviously the simpler the design, the easier it will be to cut.

POTATO CUTS

Simple patterns can be produced from potatoes. Using a knife, cut a potato in half to create a smooth printing surface. Trace a simple motif on the flat sur-face and cut away the area outside the design. Cut deeply using lino-cutting tools, a knife or a potato peeler so the furrows won't fill with paint.

To use the potato-cut, first press the potato onto newspaper several times to soak up excess moisture, then apply paint to the cut surface with a brush and stamp onto your fabric.

Quick and easy to handle, the disadvantage of the potato is that it soon perishes; it needs to be used within a twenty-four hour period. For a larger print, try cutting the design from a turnip.

WOOD PRINTING BLOCKS

Balsa wood can be purchased in assorted sizes from hobby and craft suppliers. The softness of the wood makes it a pleasure to cut and indentations can be made easily with knitting needles.

Or you can buy a length of wood and cut it down to an appropriate size for your blocks. Then glue small lids, pieces of rope, thick wire or other ordinary objects onto the blocks with impact adhesive or a two-part epoxy resin.

LINOLEUM

For more complex designs, use a linoleum square. Work on a large piece to give you more freedom of movement; it can be cut down to size after your image is cut out.

First paint the linoleum with white emulsion or acrylic to make your drawing stand out. Then draw the design onto the surface, and carefully cut away with a lino cutter (this usually has a solid wooden handle and an assortment of blades). Remember that the area left on the block will be inked and create a positive impression. After the design has been inscribed, cut the linoleum to size. Try a few trial prints to check that you have cut deep enough, and that there are no irregularities. Glue the linoleum onto a wooden block ready for use.

SPONGE PRINTS

A very simple way to add detail to plain fabric is to use a natural sponge: apply paint onto the sponge with a large flat brush and, using gentle pressure, press the sponge onto the fabric. Multi-coloured layers can be built up with a minimum of effort.

HAND-BLOCK PRINTING

Almost any object that would make an attractive print can be glued onto a wooden block.

MATERIALS
- 4cm (1 ½in) thick length of wood
- handsaw and sandpaper
- cork, curtain rings, small lids, coiled rope, bottle caps, or other small objects to make print motifs
- craft knife
- impact adhesive or two-part epoxy resin
- newspapers, thick fabric or blanket and blotting paper
- fabric
- flat, wide brush
- printing inks or acrylic paint

1 First make the printing blocks. Cut the length of wood into 4cm (1½in) cubes and lightly sand the sawn edges. Glue curtain rings, coins, bottle tops, a 'slice' of cork, coil of rope or small lid onto the surface of each wooden cube with impact adhesive or two-part epoxy resin. Leave to dry thoroughly.

2 Set up a basic printing area: this should consist of a layer of firm, thick fabric such as felt or a blanket, then a few layers of newspaper, finishing with a final layer of blotting paper.

3 Create a suitable space for drying the printed fabric, such as a simple washing line strung across the kitchen or work-room.

4 Stretch the fabric out on the printing area. For slippery material such as silk or satin, secure the edges to the work surface with drawing pins or masking tape.

5 Apply paint to the block with a flat, wide brush, then press the block on the fabric using a firm pressure. Immediately lift the block off the fabric. Apply new paint for each print. When completed, leave to dry.

These attractive fabrics exhibit the effects of hand-block printing, and designs can be small, pretty repeat patterns or larger, bolder images.

MARBLING FABRICS

Marbling is a fascinating way to produce subtle, flowing and original designs on your fabric. The process is the same as that used for paper-marbling: paint is applied to the surface of water or a gelatinous size, and a print is taken from the floating paint patterns. The control you have over the finished effect is entirely dependent on the size and on the consistency of the paints.

MARBLING TECHNIQUES

Oil-marbling is the simplest method, and requires an absolute minimum of equipment and craft skills. The technique uses oil-paints on water, and produces very exciting but unpredictable results.

Seaweed or carragheen moss-marbling is a more professional controlled method of marbling, and water-based paint is floated onto a size of boiled sea-weed gel, which thickens the water and keeps the paint from sinking. This more involved technique requires some experimentation at first, but the final results are very complex and exciting.

FABRICS

Plain cotton, silk, linen or taffeta are the ideal fabrics to use for marbling, although some intriguing effects can be produced by using patterned fabrics in spots, stripes or checks. Also consider how you will be using the finished fabric, as the marbled fabric will not be washable.

Pre-wash and dry fabric if it is brand new to make sure it is colourfast. Old pieces of fabric can be used without any advance preparation as long as they are clean. The exception is when using more complicated methods of marbling, such as seaweed marbling; in this case your fabric will have to be mordanted (meaning to fix the colours with chemicals) to keep the design colourfast.

USING PAINTS

The paints you choose depends on your marbling technique, and all the supplies you need can be purchased from art and craft suppliers.

Artists' oil paints are used for oil-marbling. Make sure you purchase the highest quality paint; inexpensive Chinese or Taiwan oil colours produce a poor finished effect. These paints need to be thinned with turpentine so the paint floats on the surface of the water or size.

Special, ready-prepared marbling paints are used for seaweed-marbling. Gouache or poster paints can also be used, but need to be thinned with distilled water until the paint is runny and smooth. Both these choices need to be mixed with ox gall.

USING DISPERSING AGENTS

Ox gall is used as a dispersing agent to help the colours spread across the surface of the size. The amount used is very critical and it is best applied with an eye dropper. Six to eight drops of ox-gall will probably be all that is needed to mix with a few table-spoons of colour. Test the mixed paint first on the size; as a rough guide, a drop of colour should expand to about 5cm (2in) on the surface of the size. Add more ox-gall if the colour doesn't spread, and bear in mind that if a new colour is dropped onto another, it will need a higher proportion of ox-gall.

Turpentine is also used as a dispersing agent to ensure the paint floats on the water surface, expanding gently. Experiment first with proportions of oil paint to turpentine to see how much turpentine you need to prevent the colour sinking to the bottom.

TRAYS AND SIZE

You will need a shallow tray for your water or size. The tray should be larger than the size of the fabric you are marbling; although enormous trays are available from garden centres, smaller ones such as cat-litter or photographic trays are perfect for your first attempt at marbling.

The elaborate swirling patterns created by marbling fabric can be bold or subdued, depending on the paint colours you choose.

OIL-MARBLING

This technique is an ideal introduction to fabric marbling, but the patterns will have to be captured quickly as the paints move rapidly.

MATERIALS
- shallow tray
- tubes of artists' oil paints
- turpentine or white spirit
- plenty of newspaper
- brushes or wooden cocktail sticks
- paint containers such as jars, lids or individual foil containers
- fabrics

1 Cover the work surface or table with a substantial layer of newspaper. Fill the tray with water. Cut strips of newspaper the width of the tray to skim off excess colour from the surface of the water after each print is taken.

2 Thin a small amount of oil paint with turpentine and drop the colour on the water. If the colour spreads over the entire tray, it may need to be mixed with a little more paint; if the colour doesn't spread enough, mix in more turpentine. Mix the correct proportion of turpentine with each colour of paint.

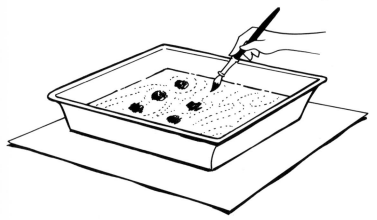

3 Drop the paints onto the water using a brush or stick, then slowly draw the colours across the surface, creating swirling movements. The colours will settle briefly into an ornate pattern, then carry on moving and changing in form as they touch each other.

4 Watch the colours until they settle into an attractive pattern. If the colours are constantly moving, they can be slowed down by adding a little wallpaper paste or powdered gelatine to the water, but make sure the mixture is completely smooth with no lumps.

5 Lay the fabric gently on the surface. To avoid air bubbles forming, roll your fabric carefully from one end onto the surface. Then immediately lift the fabric from the tray and lay the wet fabric on a thick layer of newspaper so most of the moisture is soaked up.

6 Before taking another print, skim the surface of the water with newspaper strips to remove excess paint. More paint may need to be added to the water.

7 Dry the fabric over a line or on a newspaper-covered flat surface such as the floor or a table. When completely dry, lightly iron the fabric.

Here are some excellent examples of marbled fabric. Although seaweed-marbling gives you more control over the final pattern, both techniques create lovely designs similar to Italian marbled paper.

SEAWEED-MARBLING

Although this technique is a little time-consuming, and may be one you would like to work up to, the colourful patterns hold longer and can be manipulated better than with oil-marbling.

MATERIALS
- large pan for the size
- carragheen moss or powdered extract
- fine cloth or muslin for straining
- fabric
- alum (available from a chemist)
- jug or bowl and sponge for mordanting fabric
- shallow tray
- newspaper
- ox-gall
- eye dropper
- marbling colours or gouache or poster paint mixed with distilled water
- pots, lids and palettes for mixing paints
- brushes or wooden cocktail sticks

1 First prepare the size. Stir 150g (5^1/$_4$oz) of carragheen moss into a large pan containing 8 litres (17 pints) of water and slowly bring to the boil. Boil for 5–10 minutes, then add 2 litres (3^1/$_2$ pints) of cold water.

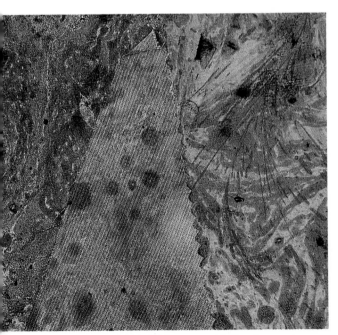

When cool, strain through a fine cloth or muslin and leave for at least 12 hours until it feels slightly gelatinous. If the size is too thick it will create concentrates of sinking colour; too thin, and it will not have enough substance to hold the colours.

2 Meanwhile, mordant the fabric. Mix 30g (1oz) of alum to 600ml (1 pint) of boiling water in a large container, stirring until it is dissolved. When cool, evenly sponge the mixture onto the entire fabric surface or dip the fabric gently in the solution. Leave to dry.

3 When the size and fabric has been prepared, cover the work surface with newspaper and cut newspaper strips the width of the tray.

4 Fill the tray with size – it should be at least 2cm (3/4in) deep. Make sure the size and paints are at room temperature; a cold size may cause colours to sink to the bottom of the tray.

5 Mix each colour of paint with ox-gall, as described on page 116.

6 Skim the surface of the size with a newspaper strip and drop your colours on evenly over the surface. Create patterns by moving the colour around, using a needle, stick or paintbrush.

7 Take a print by laying your fabric gently on the pattern, avoiding air bubbles, as described in step 5 of Oil-marbling. Then lift from the size and rinse under running water. The alum-treated fabric will hold the design, and any surplus or residue is washed away.

8 Before taking subsequent prints, or if the size has been left standing for some time, skim the surface of the size. Dry and iron the fabric as described in step 7 of Oil-marbling.

TIP
You may get better results if you flick the paint into the water with a paintbrush evenly over the surface. This creates tiny droplets of paint.

Index

Abstract: cards, 61; designs, 18, 20, 58, 61, 86
African: basketry, 29; textiles, 12
Antique: fabrics, 8, 48, 58; fairs, 8, 58

Balsa wood, 91, 92, 114
Banjara embroidery, 88
Baskets, 14, 15, 17
Beads, 58, 66, 68, 70, 74, 78, 88, 90, 91–3, 96, 97, 98; balsa wood, 92; fabric, 93; plastic, 91
Bleaching, 111–13
Borders, 48, 55–6
Bracelets, 80, 100–1
Broderie anglais, 13
Brooches, 74, 99
Buttons, 58, 66, 68, 70, 74, 88, 90, 91, 94–5, 98, 99, 100

Canvas, 22
Cellophane, 40, 41, 66, 78
Charity shops, 8, 100
Checked fabrics, 8, 29, 46, 95
Chiffon, 13, 14, 43, 68, 75, 77, 78, 100
Children's clothes, 8, 11, 68, 72, 77, 102, 106
Christmas: cards, 64–5; wreath, 82–3
Collage, 64
Comb, decoration with, 52
Crêpe, 58, 60, 62, 75, 84, 93
Cushions: woollen, 102, 104–5; woven, 40, 43
Curtain poles and rings, 48–51
Customizing clothes, 94, 102
Cutting fabrics, 16

Delaunay, Sonia, 61
Design: inspiration, 10, 18, 29; planning, 20; transferring, 20, 22
Dyeing, 66, 110–12; tie-dyeing, 112–13

Earrings, 66, 98–9
Egg cups, 80, 81, 85, 87
Eggs, 70, 71, 81, 84–5; hand-blown, 84–5
Embroidery, 62, 70, 88, 89, 91, 95, 98, 100, 102, 106, 108; silk, 74, 78, 85, 88, 89
Enamel, 80–1, 85, 86–7

Fair Isle, 11, 102, 106–8
Felt, 10, 58, 68, 70, 71, 74, 78
Floral prints, 8, 12, 29, 46, 48, 52, 55, 56, 58, 62, 77, 81, 86, 93, 95
Framing: cards, 60; weaving, 41
Furniture, 6; chair, 52–4; chest-of-drawers, 15, 52–4; stool, 44–7

Glitter glue, 41, 64, 66, 78
Greetings cards, 18, 58–9, 61, 64, 65

Hankies, 6, 8, 58, 60, 62, 66, 67, 75, 84, 85
Hessian, 27, 78
Hooks, 22, 23, 24, 38, 68

Indian fabric, 12, 18, 43, 60, 80, 111

Jewellery, 66, 68, 70, 71, 91–3, 96–101; see also separate headings
Jugs, 80, 81, 86, 87

Klee, 61
Knitwear, 10, 11, 102–9

Lace, 10, 13, 14, 28, 29, 40, 43, 64, 66, 70, 74, 77, 78, 100, 111

Marbling, 100; oil, 116, 118; seaweed, 116, 117, 119
Matisse, 61
Mondrian, 61
Mordant, 116, 119
Mounts, 60, 61, 64

Necklaces, 90, 96–7
Net, 12, 29, 43, 66, 75, 76–7, 78

Ox gall, 116, 119

Paints, 44, 52–7, 64, 65, 66, 82, 91, 94, 101, 114–15, 116–19
Paisley, 12, 13, 80
Papier mâché bowls, 88–9
Patchwork, 6, 106; blanket, 106–8; rug, 24–6
Picasso, 61
Pinboard, 62, 63
Plastic tubing, 91, 101
Plates, 81, 86–7
Postcards, 14, 18; fabric, 62–3
Printing, 110, 114–15; hand-block, 114–15; linoleum, 114; potato-cut, 114
Prodder, 27

Rag balls, 6, 14, 15, 17, 20, 24, 33, 35, 37, 38, 41, 87
Ribbons, 10, 14, 28, 29, 40, 43, 66, 68, 74, 77, 78, 88, 100
Rugs: coiled rope, 28–32; crocheted, 38–9; finishing, 23, 26, 32, 33, 34, 36, 37, 39; hooked, 6, 24–6; knitted, 37; plaited, 6, 34–6; proddy, 6, 27; rag, 6, 18; rope, 28–33; wrapped rope, 33

Rush seating, 44

Satin, 10, 12, 14, 28, 29
Scarves, 8, 13, 43, 60, 62, 75, 77, 100
Seagrass, 44, 46–7
Seaweed, 116, 119
Shells, 66, 68, 69
Silks, 13, 14, 16, 29, 60, 62, 74, 75, 78, 100
Sketchpad, 18
Sorting rags, 14
Sourcing fabrics, 8, 10–13
Sponging, 55, 56, 57, 62, 82, 94, 114
Stencils, 55–7
Storing rags, 15
Swimsuits, 13, 77

T-shirts, 8, 14, 37, 68
Tartan, 12, 60, 78, 80, 86, 95
Theatrical costumiers, 10
Ties and cravats, 13, 29, 60, 75, 100
Tray, mosaic-effect, 82

Weaving: loom, 41–2; shuttle, 42; hanging, 42
Wreaths: bases, 66; Christmas, 82–3; hanky, 67, 75; heart, 71–5; knit, 72–3; seaside, 66, 68–9; tropical, 76–7

Varnishing, 81

Acknowledgements

The author would like to thank all her friends for their generous contributions of old clothes and fabrics, especially Emma and Lindsay Phillips, Judith Higginbottom, Kathryn Sinclair, Shelagh Weeks and Veronica Mills. A special thank you to Alice Reeves for her woven cushion and stool, Sara Tempany for Christmas hearts and Lindsay Phillips for her Christmas card inspiration. To Alex Kirk and Patrick Reeves for help with cutting rags, Gordon West for a lifetime's supply of inspirational books and a word processor, and Rob Reeves for copious cups of coffee and endless patience. I would like to extend a special thank you to Di Lewis for all the lovely photographs and her enthusiastic appreciation of the projects.

The publishers would also like to thank Ann Davies for the loan of the proddy rug featured on page 27.